CONTENTS

INTRODUCTION

ROACH, rudd and dace are readily caught by the same techniques, on identical tackle and baits, often from the same locations, and in truth the angler is never quite sure which species will bite next. It therefore seemed that to combine all three in one volume would help the angler rather than distract. Indeed, during the structuring of this book what became apparent immediately was that scarcely is there a method, a technique or a bait that will not catch these diminutive, yet favourite species.

Sadly, a number of today's young fishermen will neither share, nor even understand, my undying love of the roach. To those who specialize only in pike fishing, it is just another bait, and with so many stillwaters now prolifically stocked with carp, the attraction of hitting into large, hard-fighting fish does rather make catching even a 1 lb roach or rudd seem second rate. To my mind this is a great pity because the skills one needs to master in order to be successful at catching roach, rudd and dace will stand the fisherman in good stead to extract carp, and even pike, from fisheries anywhere in the world. The finesse and techniques involved should not be overlooked. They incorporate the basis for continual success and enjoyment, plus no small understanding of the natural history below the surface of both still and flowing waters, guaranteed to last you through an entire lifetime's fishing.

CHAPTER ONE

ABOUT ROACH

ROACH
(Rutilus rutilus)

The roach has the distinction of being the most commonly caught freshwater fish within the British Isles, and a species indigenous to England, although it has become far more widespread in recent decades (see Distribution, p. 13). Roach are indeed blessed with the classical 'fish form'. A smooth, rounded body, distinctly oval in cross-section, with a short head and small mouth. The lips when open are level, compared with the lower lip of the rudd, which protrudes (see Hybrids, p. 12).

Colouration can vary tremendously from summer to winter, and especially from one environment to another. Clear-water roach, for instance, are far more brightly coloured, and have a minimal layer of protective mucus, whereas those inhabiting coloured waters produce a noticeably thicker layer of slime and are much paler in overall colouration. There is usually, however, a dark grey-greenish sheen along the back, fusing into silvery flanks, where the lateral line is most noticeable. The belly is always a creamy white. The scales are relatively large, certainly much larger than those of the dace or bream of equal size, and covered in bright reflective enamel, which is more intense in young roach.

During the winter months, when water temperatures are low, there is a distinct blue tinge to each scale along the upper sides and back, whereas in the summer the overall colouration is rather brassy. The pectoral fins have the least amount of colour, being a translucent warm grey-brown, while the pectoral and anal fins show more warmth in tones of muted orange or red. The dorsal and tail, which is deeply forked, are both more darkly coloured and tinged in crimson. Whenever a mystery fish porpoises momentarily prolific of our indigenous cyprinid species, creating massive shoals to secure its continued existence.

Given the right circumstances, roach will freely inter-breed with both bream and rudd when they arrive on the spawning grounds at the same time. Roach/bream hybrids are a fine-looking and most desirable fish to catch, combining the fast, dogged fight of a big roach with the slab-sided resistance and weight of the bream. I have taken them to over 5 lb from my local gravel pits in Norfolk, and of course the Norfolk Broads and their interconnecting system of tidal rivers are renowed for the fine shoals of roach/bream hybrids they contain, often averaging over 2 lb apiece. However, just to confuse the issue, hybridization does not always produce a fish that appears to be halfway between each species. The most prominent giveaway signs are the much paler body colouration and drab fins that are almost completely lacking in red pigment. The mouth is usually slightly protrusible, although some hybrids do have almost level lips, like true roach. The scales will, however, seem rather odd because in size they are smaller than those of the roach, yet larger than the bream's. The best indication of all is the hybrid's longer, bream-like anal fin, often coloured along the outside edge with a band of black (see also roach/rudd hybrids, p. 17).

DISTRIBUTION

The roach is common throughout the continent of Europe, from the brackish waters of the Caspian Sea in the east, to Yugoslavia in the south, Scandinavia in the north and Ireland in the west.

Once absent from Irish waters, the roach is now abundant throughout Ireland's major river systems, including the Blackwater, the Erne, the Shannon and the River Bann that feeds massive Lough Neagh, the largest lake in the British Isles. While roach are far from common in Devon, Cornwall and western Wales, in southern Scotland the species is well represented in Loch Lomond and in Perthshire's River Tay, where the tidal reaches are prolific in roach stocks. Elsewhere in England, almost without exception, the roach is the most common river fish.

CHAPTER TWO

ABOUT RUDD

RUDD
(Scardinius erythrophthalmus)

Despite having a fancier Latin name and being slightly slimmer than the roach in cross-section, the rudd is not totally dissimilar to the roach in body shape. The main difference, when viewed side on, is a characteristic angled 'keel' between its vent and tail root. In addition, the rudd's dorsal fin, which is set noticeably further back, overlaps the anal fin on a vertical line when folded, whereas that of the roach does not.

The real difference between the two species is the herring-like, up-turned mouth of the rudd. Its bottom jaw protrudes at an upwards angle, suggesting what most anglers quickly find out, that the rudd is built for surface feeding and intercepting falling food particles, although it also readily accepts baits presented on the bottom. And if these features are not sufficient to distinguish between the two species, in colouration the rudd wins hands down and is, without question, the most beautiful of all our freshwater fish.

Resplendent in the brightest livery, its fins are orange-scarlet, while the scales along the flank, if anything slightly larger than those of the roach, are lacquered in the most reflective, burnished, buttery gold enamel imaginable. So reflective are the rudd's scales that a tip for photographing them in bright sunshine is to always underexpose by one full stop. Otherwise your photo could easily be over-exposed. The back is brassy bronze, often with a distinct green hue in adolescent rudd. The brightest and most colourful rudd I have ever caught came from the fast, clear-flowing waters of Denmark's River Guden, and here lies a peculiarity of the species' character.

Most English anglers think of the rudd preferring the

Weighing a shade under 3 lb, this beautiful fish caught on float-fished sweetcorn from a local gravel pit is a fine specimen. Its golden, buttery yellow colouration is typical of the true rudd.

slow-moving rivers and Broads of East Anglia – shallow, weedy estate lakes, fertile, well-established gravel pits and meres, and so on. In short, everywhere except fast-running water. Yet in Denmark and in many rivers in southern Ireland, the rudd proliferates in large shoals and grows to specimen proportions in quite strong currents.

There is, however, a factor common to all waters where rudd flourish best, whether flowing or still; they are clean, weedy, chemical-free environments, unaffected by excessive eutrophication, where a healthy natural balance of aquatic insects and plants still exists. And this, in my opinion, is why this beautiful species is currently on the decline in so many English fisheries – my local Norfolk Broads are a prime example – where rudd were once common throughout the system.

Golden rudd

Though perhaps difficult to comprehend, this interesting variant is actually more intensely coloured than the common rudd. The salmon pink colouring along its back enables it to be seen easily from overhead in the clear, filtered water of garden ponds, and this is the sole reason for this variant being developed. The golden rudd is bred specifically for the pond-fish trade and is imported into the

UK from North America and Germany. Nevertheless, it has found its way into isolated angling waters and freely interbreeds with indigenous rudd, adding a touch of mystery and an extra splash of colour. It grows to nowhere near such large proportions, and a golden rudd of 1 lb plus should be considered a fine specimen.

FEEDING

A strange feeding characteristic of the rudd is that invariably shoal members all tend to be more or less of the same size and of the same year or spawning class. You can catch stunted rudd from small farm ponds and irrigation reservoirs, all 4 or 5 in long, one after another, and from an estate lake or reed-fringed mere specimen rudd averaging just below and just above the 2 lb mark, with only 1–2 oz separating them. Crucian carp are known for a similar phenomenon. I am not sure whether it is a case of varying-sized fish not fairing well together as a family shoal, because one class tends to dominate the available food source; or simply that only one particular year class is actually present in the swim at any one time. In any event, it is a phenomenon to bear in mind wherever you fish for rudd.

Rudd being a shoal fish, much that I have already mentioned about roach also applies to it, especially the importance of light values, because rudd also commence feeding with real aggression and far less caution under the cloak of dusk when the surface is littered with hatching flies. They also sometimes respond in reverse to light values by becoming active at midday when the sun is at its highest point and the surface water layers that much warmer. Indeed, the rudd more than any other is the fish of summer, as anyone seeking to catch them in really cold winter weather soon appreciates. In winter often they only become active enough to accept your bait an hour or so either side of midday when light penetration through the cold water is at its highest.

Their dietary requirements demand a regular supply of hatching aquatic insects within the upper water layers, particularly midges and sedges, and zooplankton such as

daphnia. Rudd also eat crustaceans and other bottom-
dwellers, and an amount of vegetable matter. They seem
particularly partial to the algae growing on reed stems.

Rudd have a slightly greater weight potential than
roach, the British record being a 4 lb 8 oz specimen caught
way back in 1933 by the late Rev. E. C. Alston from a
mere near Thetford, Norfolk. For a short time this
exceptionally old-established record was replaced on the
list by a fish 2 oz heavier caught on a nymph from Pitsford
Reservoir in Northamptonshire in 1986 by Mr D. Webb
when fly-fishing for trout. However, at a later date his
catch was judged to be a rudd/roach hybrid and deleted,
and the Rev. Alston's Norfolk rudd was reinstated.

This chain of events highlights two points: firstly, how
even experts have difficulty distinguishing between rudd/
roach hybrids (the British Record Fish Committee no less),
and secondly, how susceptible rudd are to artificial flies.
Reservoirs like Pitsford, well known for its prolific stocks
of rudd (and roach), offers wonderful specimen fish
potential to those bent on catching monster rudd with the
fly rod. While presenting a slow-sinking nymph in the
upper water layers would seem the best technique, big
Pitsford rudd are often caught on large, fry-imitating
attractor flies of 2–3 in in length. Like most cyprinids,
when massive fry shoals pack tightly together (a ready
food source) adult rudd become cannibalistic and regularly
chomp into their own offspring (see Fly-fishing, p. 125).

REPRODUCTION AND HYBRIDS

Rudd move onto the weedy shallows to spawn at some
time during the very same April to June period in which
roach and bream also endeavour to propagate their species.
The tiny, pinkish, translucent eggs adhere to whatever
medium is available at the time; soft weeds, rush and reed
stems, submerged marginal grasses, fibrous tree roots,
etc., and take from 10 to 12 days to hatch.

Although rudd sometimes spawn slightly later than the
roach, inevitably where all three species are present in a
river or stillwater, rudd/roach hybrids, rudd/bream and
roach/bream are all a very real possibility. I have already

*Even experts have
great difficulty in
distinguishing
between roach and
rudd. If you are in any
doubt whatsoever, call
it a hybrid, as indeed
this 2 lb plus beauty,
taken by long trotting
from a Norfolk stream
by Andy Jubb, proved
to be.*

described what to look for in a roach/bream hybrid (see p. 13), and owing to the obvious golden rudd-like sheen along its flanks, a rudd/bream hybrid is not difficult to identify.

Strangely, rudd/bream hybrids are far from common in England and in my home county of Norfolk I can only ever recall identifying rudd/bream hybrids from one particular water, a deep, reed-fringed mere, where roach, rudd and bream are all prolific. This lack of rudd/bream hybrids in England has always puzzled me, because in southern Ireland, in river systems like the mighty Shannon, rudd/bream are very common and grow to a large size – 5 lb and over. They are splendid-looking creatures and are much prized for their hard-fighting qualities, and certainly not looked down upon, which sadly is the attitude of some anglers with regard to hybrids. Why, I cannot comprehend.

The rudd/roach hybrid, as I have already suggested, really does cause the most confusion, and even arguments, between anglers. Many such hybrids look remarkably like a true rudd or a true roach. Some will have the extended bottom lip of the rudd, but a considerably paler body colour when compared to the rich, buttery gold of a true rudd, while others will be roach-like in colouration with a noticeable rudd-like angle or keel between the tail root and vent. The lips vary anywhere between level and the bottom one fully protruding.

The best way to approach the subject is firstly to enjoy the fight and physical being of such a lovely fish, especially if it is a specimen, and then if in any doubt whatsoever as to its parentage, simply call it a hybrid. I, for one, would like to see the British Record Fish Committee set out separate record status for hybrids, as they are always having to deal with hybrid claims purported initially to be either true roach or rudd. Such a step would add enormous interest, and increase the number of categories for ratification.

DISTRIBUTION

Just like the roach, rudd are common throughout most of Europe, even in southern Scandinavia. Although it is quite rare in Scotland, Ireland, especially the south, offers superlative rudd fishing for both quality and quantity in just about every stillwater and river system. It is indeed far more widely distributed than the roach.

As I have hinted already, it is a sad fact that due to the species' intolerance of doctored waters (chemical and farming pollution) the rudd is nowhere near so widespread in England as it once was. It nevertheless still seems to flourish in reed-fringed meres and in man-made pits, lakes, reservoirs and especially in estate lakes. And to a much lesser extent, in canals and slow-moving rivers.

CHAPTER THREE

ABOUT DACE

DACE
(Leuciscus leuciscus)

With a galaxy of exciting and acrobatic sports fish on their doorstep, small wonder North American fishermen find difficulty in understanding our love for the humble dace. Certainly it hasn't the strength to really bang the rod over hard, nor leaves the water in a spray of foam. Yet this, the smallest of fish taken seriously by British anglers, is a firm favourite with pleasure fishermen and match anglers alike, because summer or winter it bites freely, providing an interesting challenge on light tackle.

What I like most of all about dace fishing is that many of the rivers that hold them, and where they grow largest, are pretty little rivers and beautiful chalkstreams meandering through picturesque farmlands where you can enjoy a peaceful day's sport roaming from swim to swim carrying the absolute minimum of tackle, whether wielding a float rod, a quivertip rod or a light fly rod.

Optimum weight for the dace is less than $1\frac{1}{2}$ lb. The British record weighed 1 lb $4\frac{1}{2}$ oz and was caught by J. L. Gasson from the Little Ouse near Thetford, Norfolk, in 1960. In reality, however, any dace of 10 oz upwards is a most worthy catch, and wherever dace abound in huge shoals in our larger rivers, such as the Thames or Great Ouse, an average size of somewhere between 3 and 6 oz is more likely.

The dace has a slim, rounded, smooth body with small, flat-lying scales, small head and a neat mouth. Along the back, colouration is grey-olive blending into flanks of silver enamel, the belly being matt white. The forked tail and dorsal fin are both a translucent grey, while the pectorals, pelvics and the anal fin vary from dull yellow to pale pink.

The outer edge of both its dorsal and anal fins are concave, as opposed to those of the chub, which are convex. So there should never really be any confusion between small chub and dace. Length for length, the chub's mouth is, of course, twice the size, and its colouration brassy compared to the distinct silver of the dace. With the dace a vertical line can be drawn at the front edge of both its dorsal and its pelvic fins, whereas the chub's dorsal starts in a vertical line midway along the pelvic fins.

FEEDING

The natural food eaten by dace consists of all forms of aquatic insect life, from nymphs that spend the best part of their yearly (or two-yearly) cycle crawling about on the river-bed, to the rising and hatching pupa, to the adult fly that dances on the surface. Throughout the summer their splashy rises can be seen whenever there is a good hatch of flies coming off. They also eat shrimps and even small molluscs. Their pharyngeal teeth are well developed, consisting of two rows of five large and two or three small respectively, on each plate. With such an armoury in the back of its throat, small wonder that adult dace can maul and send back to you even a large lobworm so chewed and split, you would assume the culprit a chub.

Then again, and just like the roach, in low water temperatures that coincide with clear water conditions, educated, well-fished dace can be exasperatingly choosey over a single caster in which a size 20 hook is hidden, returning merely the barest remnants of its shell with hardly a dip of the float tip as evidence. Generally speaking, however, the dace has an even more catholic taste in food than both roach and rudd. For instance, I have often taken large dace on cheese paste or big lobs (on size 8 and 6 hooks, too) while freelining for chub in the clear water of overgrown streams. Yet the roach occupying the very same swims have not been the slightest bit interested, preferring maggots and bread flake, and only responding to smelly baits during high floodwater conditions (see Baits, p. 75).

REPRODUCTION

The dace is not unlike the European ide or silver orfe, whose beautiful cousin, the golden orfe, is so loved by pond-keepers. In fact, the dace shares a peculiarity with orfe in that only prior to and during the spawning season, when the males develop hundreds of tiny tubercles over their bodies and are decidedly 'rough' to the touch, is it possible to differentiate between the sexes.

Dace spawn earlier than most species of coarse fish, usually in April. There is actually a pre-spawning segregation of the sexes during February and March. The noticeably slimmer, wiry males, now sandpapery to the touch, gather in their hundreds in the turbulent runs while the deep-chested, spawn-laden females remain in deep, slower swims until the time is ready for them to amalgamate on the fast, gravel shallows where the pinky-orange coloured eggs are laid, usually under the cloak of darkness. It is interesting to note that when dace have deposited their eggs, gestation can take up to three weeks – at least twice that of most other species. This is probably due to the fact that they spawn at a time when water temperatures are lower.

Opposite *Dace may be small, but being willing to bite almost regardless of weather severity, they provide wonderful sport to the float fisherman in particular.*

DISTRIBUTION

The dace has a more easterly distribution than both roach and rudd, existing throughout much of Europe and even stretching into Asia. It is common throughout England in both slow and fast-flowing rivers, but absent from western Wales and Scotland. It has been introduced into a few rivers in southern Ireland where, like the roach, it is slowly spreading.

CHAPTER FOUR

LOCATION

FIGURE 1 *Locating roach and dace in overgrown streams and small rivers*

THERE is a charming little backstream of the River Yare not 6 miles from my house where, on almost any day during the summer, a couple of maggots or casters trotted slowly along beneath light float tackle will produce fish after fish. Not monsters by any means, but specifically roach, rudd and dace, all three species living happily together, occupying the same attractive narrow and shallow run between beds of sweet reed grass. The point I am trying to make is that very often in the case of roach and dace, or roach and rudd, two species will choose the identical habitat. And as in my favourite little backwater, all three can live in harmony. Indeed, this is one of the problems you will undoubtedly encounter when trying to locate any one of these three species.

Each does, however, have particular preferences in regard to water clarity, depth, speed of flow, aquatic plants, and so on, and in so far as this chapter is concerned, I shall relate various types of habitat to individual species, starting with the ultimate delight of flowing water in miniature.

OVERGROWN STREAMS AND SMALL RIVERS

Dace

Diminutive rivers and streams that twist and wind through rich farmland are usually full of character and thus easy to read (see fig. 1). Where the water runs sparklingly clear through beds of lush vegetation and over a gravel or sandy bed, expect to find the dace. During the summer, search through polaroid sunglasses along the shallow straights

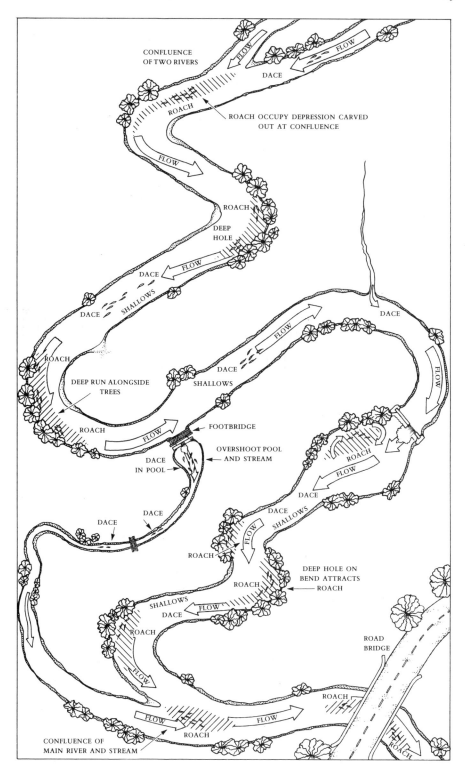

A mixture of stealth and concealment, plus a knowledge of natural baits, is the key to catching roach and dace inhabiting overgrown streams and small rivers during the summer months.

between bends, at the tail ends of small weir-pools or hatches, in the fast junction runs where carriers merge with the main course, even in tiny side streams and ditches narrow enough to be jumped, in water from a mere 6 to 24 in deep. Walk stealthily and keep low to the marginal cover, trying not to cast your shadow over the surface, and the dace will bite freely.

During the coldest weeks of the winter the larger, female dace will retreat into the secluded holes on bends and into the deep back eddies of weir or overshoot pools. And when the little river is in full rip-roaring spate and the colour of strong tea, both male and female dace, together with roach, chub and even the odd trout, will all pack into slacks immediately downstream of acute bends where the flow is least forceful and the water carrying less debris. When the floods recede and the level returns to normal, back the dace will go to their preferred shallows.

The largest dace of all come from the pure water of southern chalksteams like the upper reaches of the rivers Avon, Test, Kennet and Windrush, which all have two important factors in common – a rich, abundant larder of aquatic insects, combined with a relatively low fish density. Many of the choicest stretches are, in fact, stocked with trout and thus regularly electro-fished to remove the coarse species. So those remaining grow very large indeed.

Needless to say, in stretches of chalkstreams or in the

When the main river is out of sorts, running high and coloured, search for roach in quieter water, like overshoot pools and side streams, where they can be caught by trotting at quite close range during mild conditions, or by stret pegging in low temperatures.

larger rivers that breed really huge shoals of dace, the average size is bound to be very much smaller. It is all about supply and demand in the food stakes.

Roach

The same can be said about the roach inhabiting overgrown streams and small rivers. Locate a small shoal in a rich environment lacking other roach and additional competition

The roach shoals in wide, deep rivers keep close to the bottom during the winter months. John used the pole to ease maggots slowly along the bottom beneath an 8 g float to take this mint-conditioned roach from the mighty River Bann in Northern Ireland.

species, and each individual has the potential to reach
specimen proportions, perhaps 2 lb and over. Not so with
the members of a shoal numbering hundreds, or in the case
of big river shoals numbering several hundreds, or even
thousands. Individual size is always governed by the
available food source and, of course, the fish's age.

Roach generally prefer more water over their backs than
dace, and of a slower pace. Through clear water, look for
them hugging the bottom in all the deeper runs, especially
in holes on the bends and those close into the bank where
overhanging foliage shades the surface from strong sun-
light. Confluences where the continual force of merging
currents keep a long, deepish run free of tangles and silt,
bringing the shoal a regular supply of food particles, are at
the very top of the list. Roach also feel happy in deep weir-
pools and in lay-bys, which afford the shoal immediate rest
from the full current force. And they love long, even-
paced glides immediately downstream from an acute bend.
They hate turbulence where the flow switches direction
every few seconds, so when roach are not visible (as they
are in the summer) learn to study surface currents,
immediately ignoring swims where spirals of water
continually spew up to the surface. Opt for steady water if
you wish to catch small river roach with any degree of
consistency, especially throughout the cold winter months,
when their metabolic rate slows down, making them far
less keen to chase their food.

BIG RIVERS

Dace

To find dace in larger, deeper rivers, look for stretches or
smaller areas within a long reach where the flow is
noticeably faster. Such swims occur whenever the river
narrows, thus forcing the flow along at a faster pace. Weir-
pools always attract dace like bees to a honey pot, right at
the end of each flush in the well-oxygenated, bubbly
water, and invariably at the very tail end of the pool,
where the bottom shelves up and the water glides over
gravel runs separated by flowing weedbeds. Whenever the

flow is increased by the extra water from sidestreams converging with the main river, dace will almost certainly be in residence. In fact, at virtually any junction or run, where dissolved oxygen levels are increased by an extra push of water, you can expect dace to be at home.

It is fair to say, and this may seem contradictory, that large shoals of dace may also be found in the slow, deep stretches of certain rivers in the company of roach shoals. Rivers that immediately spring to mind are the middle to lower reaches of the Thames and Great Ouse, where catches often consist of equal numbers of both dace and roach from the same swim. The species is very adaptable and it stands to reason that every dace in the river cannot hope to occupy the choicest spots. The greatest concentrations will, however, always be found in the faster, shallower reaches.

Roach

During the summer in low water levels and slow currents, the roach shoals of larger rivers tend to spread out and might be found almost anywhere, from the cabbage patches along the marginal shelf, which provide a wealth of natural food and cover from predators, to the bubbly water of large weir-pools (see fig. 2).

Roach can often be seen porpoising on the surface at dawn and again at dusk, pinpointing their exact location to the enthusiast throughout the entire season except in sub-zero conditions. Once the summer weeds have rotted away, the shoals, feeling naked and vulnerable, tend to group together and move into the choicest swims. As they do in overgrown streams, the roach of larger rivers predictably select runs where the flow is steady. If there is the choice of protection overhead, such as a road or train bridge, or a line of overhanging willows or alders, then so much the better. The shoal may even happily exist in a relatively shallow swim. Generally, however, the pointers to look for are long runs, say from 5 to 10 ft deep, beyond the marginal shelf where the flow is steady.

All deep, slow eddies in weir-pools are potential roach hot-spots, as are those last few hundred yards of the river immediately above a weir or mill pool where the flow

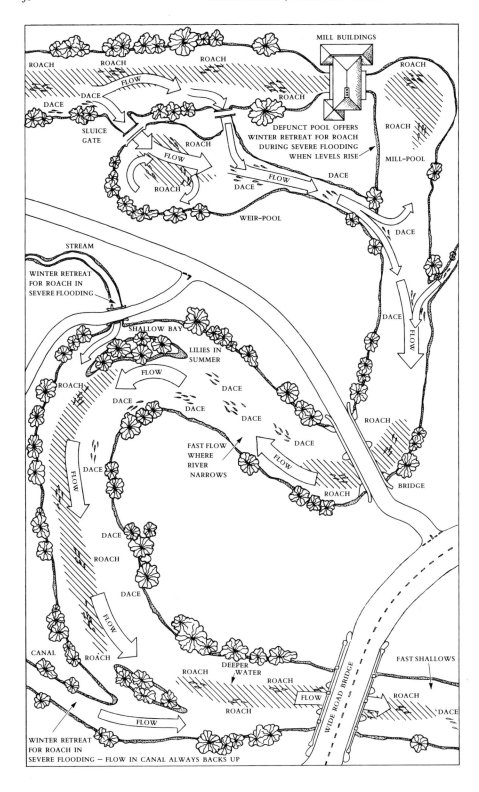

smooths down, particularly at the back-end of the season from mid-February until mid-March. I am not sure why, but large concentrations of roach tend to pack into these spots at this time.

FIGURE 2 *Locating dace and roach in big rivers*

Never ignore shallow backwaters and sidestreams that join the river and which, during the clear water of summer, are full of weed and fry shoals. At flood time, especially when the main river is 3 or 4 ft up and heavily coloured, roach pack like sardines into these havens and provide fabulous sport.

It is most important to become familiar with the river's character and its topography; something only hard work with the plummet and reconnaissance trips with polaroid glasses during the summer months will achieve. In short, you should find out the depths and length (before it shallows up) of each holding run worth considering a roach swim. You should also know the exact whereabouts of snags, undercut banks, sandbars, gravel runs and weedbeds, and especially those spots where large con-centrations of pike love to lie in wait. You do not necessarily need to be wary of them, although repeated attacks on fish being played does bring out the worst in us all, but wherever there are numbers of pike in a roach river, there will be large shoals of roach near by. The two go hand in hand. In fact, many a morning's pike fishing, roaming the river with a spinning rod, has allowed me to pinpoint potential roach hot-spots for future attention.

Rudd

To the best of my knowledge, while the rudd is not prolific in any large river in England, as I have already mentioned, rudd are common throughout most of the river systems in southern Ireland – even the larger, deep and often fast rivers like the mighty Shannon. Like roach, rudd, too, give away their position by porpoising at dawn and again at dusk during the summer, and may be taken at almost any depth from just beneath the surface to just above bottom in up to 20 ft of water. Generally speaking, however, they are more commonly located immediately beyond the marginal shelf, among the covering of yellow water-lilies or beside clumps of bullrushes.

PONDS

Roach and rudd

FIGURE 3 *Locating*
roach and rudd in
estate lakes

It is quite possible with two ponds of identical size and character, situated not far apart, that one will contain roach and the other rudd. A third in close proximity might contain a mixture of both species, and this is far more likely. In shallow and thus warm little ponds that turn pea green during the summer, both species breed so prolifically they become over-populated. With a limited food source the fish become stunted (unless a head of predators are present or introduced) and incredibly easy to catch, whether you present your bait just below the surface or on the bottom, in the edge under the rod-tip or bang in the middle. Quite simply, like currants in a well-baked cake, they are layered evenly and everywhere in the water.

It may be coincidence, but in my home county of Norfolk I have noticed that in small, deep ponds or pits with depths of 10 ft or more, there is a chance that a few of the roach may find enough surplus natural food eventually to top 1 lb in weight. In really shallow, confined waters, on the other hand, the rudd would seem to have a better chance of producing one or two larger-than-average specimens.

ESTATE LAKES AND MERES

Rudd

In my opinion, rudd fair best of all, and usually grow to specimen proportions, in meres and the kind of rich and weedy clear-water habitat created by damming streams meandering through prime farmland. Estate lakes, as I shall call them, all follow a similar simple format (fig. 3). They are shallow one end, where rich silt beds form due to sediment brought down by the feeder stream, and increase in depth gradually towards the dam wall at the other end.

In the summer, rudd feed among the shallows from the surface on hatching midges, whose larvae, the blood-

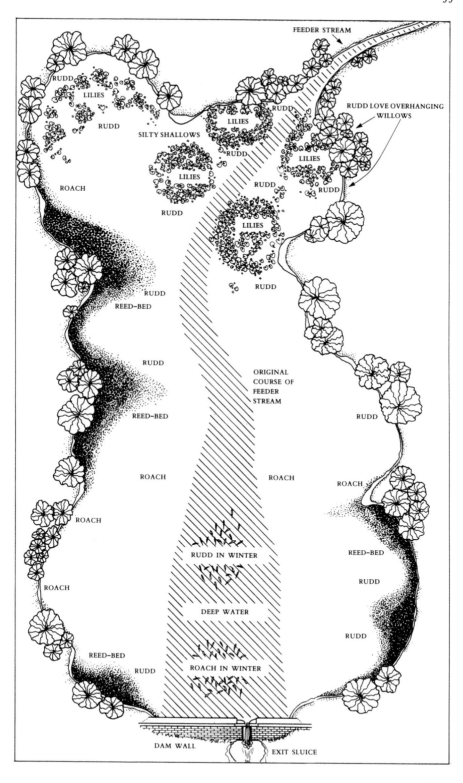

Nestling in picturesque valleys and lined around the margins with reed-beds and overhanging trees and with the surface covered in patches of lilies, the clear water of estate lakes provide the best rudd habitat of all. Concentrate on the shallows during the summer and in the deeper water close to the dam in the winter.

worm, live by the million in the layers of rich organic silt. And in winter they tend to shoal up tightly in the deepest water by the dam itself. Rudd love the shade provided by over-hanging willows and extensive beds of water-lilies, whether fringing the margins or planted way out in the middle. Look through binoculars and you will observe the pads shake as rudd pick off snails and their eggs from the undersides. They also love to patrol and work along tall reedbeds, feeding on insects and algae clinging to the stems, which can be seen 'knocking' together on a perfectly still day.

Even estate lakes that contain few predators and are over-populated with rudd still produce a large enough larder of natural food for the adult rudd to average out at somewhere between 6 and 12 oz, plus the occasional one over 1 lb. And in those lakes where numbers of both perch and pike exist, the average size of the rudd might easily top 1 lb, with the occasional year class or group weighing well in excess of 2 lb.

Roach

While roach never really seem able to capitalize as much as rudd on the available natural food supply, when sharing even moderate-sized estate lakes, they do breed most prolifically. I know of numerous estate lakes in East Anglia stocked only with roach, which really do offer superlative

When searching small rivers for roach and dace during the colder months of winter, concentrate on feature swims, lay-bys, acute bends, and the point where carriers or side streams merge with the main flow.

sport, both winter and summer, with quality fish averaging between 4 and 10 oz. Very rarely does anything larger turn up, however.

During the winter months the shoals vacate the marginal shallows for the protection of deeper water, and invariably pack very tightly together in close proximity to the dam itself. Pick a mild spell and you could enjoy a netful.

IRRIGATION DRAINS AND CANALS

Rudd

Among a rich habitat of lilies covering the surface, coupled to thick beds of reeds or rushes along the margins, is where you are most likely to encounter the rudd of the shallow and sluggish Cambridgeshire and Lincolnshire drains. They are most prolific in systems that remain clear for much of the season, and which contain extensive beds of bottom-rotted plants such as Canadian pond-weed, millfoil and hornwort.

The same can be said of defunct, overgrown canals, even those not particularly rich in aquatic plants, which appear barren with made-up banks for mile upon mile. Find a lone patch of lilies or a strip of sweet reed grass spreading out

FIGURE 4 *Locating*
roach and rudd in
gravel pits

across the water on its own rootstock, and if there are any
rudd present, you will have located them.

Roach

While drain and canal roach tend to be widespread during
the warmer months and spread across from bank to bank,
once cold weather really sets in they pack tightly together
close to the bottom along the centre channel, where the
depth is greatest. This results in long stretches of water
being almost devoid of fish. Then, quite suddenly, several
yards or more of the middle basin is crammed with roach.

Roach usually give away their presence in these veritable
hot-spots during all but the most severe winter weather by
topping on the surface as dawn breaks. However, as this
surface activity may last no longer than a few minutes, it
pays to be there early in order to capitalize on the ritual.

GRAVEL PITS

Roach and rudd

The best roach and rudd fishing exists in well-established
and mature old gravel-workings, in particular those
excavated during World War II, which, through the build-
up of silt from leaves from surrounding trees and aquatic
plant breakdown, have over the years developed an
exceptionally rich and abundant food source (fig. 4).

Rudd, if present, are more prolific and grow to a good
average size in pits where the gravel seams were shallow,
resulting in irregular bottom contours and large areas of
weedy, shallow water interspersed with tree-clad islands.
Roach much prefer the larger, more open pits, which
provide a consistently good depth of 8 ft and more. Those
that contained long, deep seams of gravel prior to
excavation, result in deep holes and gullies capable of
holding massive roach stocks. In many such pits, the depth
plummets to 10 ft or more just beyond the marginal shelf,
and in these quality roach can be taken on float tackle all
season through.

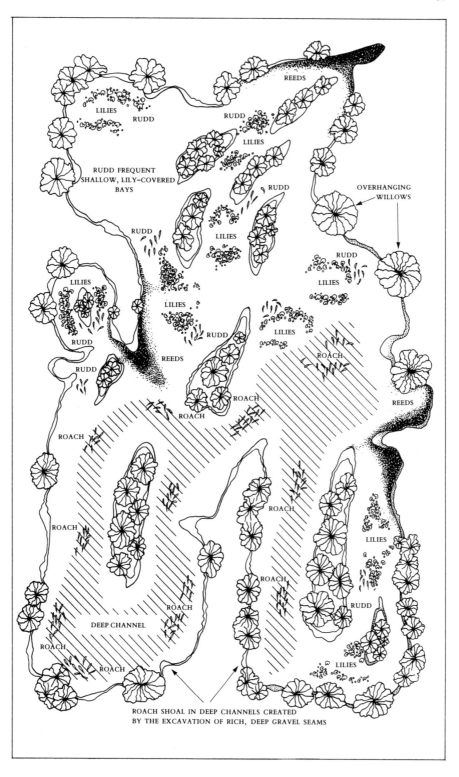

ROACH SHOAL IN DEEP CHANNELS CREATED
BY THE EXCAVATION OF RICH, DEEP GRAVEL SEAMS

As always and almost everywhere, roach and rudd living in gravel pits give away their position at dawn and again at dusk by porpoising on the surface. I know I have said it before, and I shall most certainly keep repeating the worth of actually being at the water as dawn breaks. I know of no more accurate method of location than observing several fish topping on the surface, and then casting to that same spot.

RESERVOIRS AND HUGE LAKES

Rudd and roach

I would include many of the Irish loughs and lakes when contemplating rudd and roach location in huge stillwaters, because the very same principles apply to both. Indeed, all large expanses of water seem rather inhibiting at first sight, especially with a good chop on the surface. However, by systematically breaking each down into smaller areas based on different habitats or features, the task becomes easier.

In huge natural lakes, for instance, pinpoint the largest beds of common reeds or lilies skirting shallow bays and you will have found rudd. Watch, too, for their splashy rises during that last hour of evening light, when they furrow the surface sucking in hatching flies, sedges and the like. As they are never slow to move with their food source, when huge clouds of daphnia, for instance, drift with the surface tow to a particular shoreline, rudd will be there, avidly consuming vast quantities until the wind changes direction. In this situation, small amounts of loose feed catapulted regularly around the float are the only attraction required.

One of the best means of location is attraction, and a ruse that works especially well when you are afloat on a large water (because you then have the means to follow the shoal) is to scatter a pint of floating casters over the surface and watch from afar through binoculars. Once rudd find the free meal and start feeding in earnest, row quietly up to within a long float cast, and keep the shoal interested by catapulting out extra casters every so often (see Surface fishing, p. 104).

Owing to their rich, prolific food supply, deep gravel pits, lakes and reservoirs hold the largest concentrations of stillwater roach, like this beauty caught on quivertipped maggot by Martin Founds.

In vast man-made reservoirs where great depths exist, particularly at the dam end, make a point of seeking out the shallowest, weediest bays and inlets if you want summer rudd. For roach, explore areas of medium depths during the summer months by keeping an eye on the surface for rolling fish, switching attention to the deepest swims when really cold weather sets in and there are few visual pointers.

Any area that becomes popular with pike fishermen and which regularly produces for them may very well produce roach for you. Keep a watchful eye for grebes and cormorants that repeatedly work the same areas. These fishermen, remember, must catch to exist.

CHAPTER FIVE

TACKLE

WITH perhaps the exception of super-lightweight carbon poles, specialist tackle is not required to enjoy catching these three species. Moreover, as the rods, for instance, used for catching roach are exactly the same as for dace and rudd fishing, there is little point in confusing the issue. All tackle items dealt with in this chapter, therefore, apply equally to roach, rudd and dace. The only difference, of course, is in the application of technique.

RODS

Float rods

To present the bait close in, and for tackling small waters (overgrown streams, especially), my choice would be a 12-footer. Conversely, to present the bait way out into deep water with a fixed float, a 14-ft model will pick up more line on the strike and thus convert far more bites into hooked fish. However, I must admit to using a 13-footer for something like 90 per cent of my float fishing, and so I will suggest that you follow the same course if you are uncertain about length and can afford only one rod.

Choice of action in float rods is between the snappy yet easy waggler action or a fast-tip action, which has a considerably finer tip section of somewhere between 20 and 24 in spliced into the top joint. Both models are perfect for use with reel lines of between 2 and 2½ lb.

Spliced-tip rods allow for a more sensitive, delicate approach when you are underarm casting at close range and for easing the bait downstream when stick-float fishing with ultra-fine hook lengths and tiny hooks. If you can afford both actions, then fine. If not, opt for a waggler-style rod, which should prove more versatile overall, taking both close and long-range techniques into account.

Weight is a factor to consider in a rod that you could be holding all day long, and there is an enormous selection of modern lightweight float rods (also called match and bottom rods) from which to choose. Recommended manufacturers who specialize in this field are Daiwa, Ryobi, Shimano and Shakespeare. I much prefer those slim in profile, which cut easily through wind resistance and are extremely fast on the strike – a quality much needed when striking the shy bites that roach, rudd and dace can give at times.

Top manufacturers have developed various elements, such as micro whiskers of silicon carbide, that are fused into the basic rod-tube of carbon fibre in order to maintain the strength and rigidity of the slim-profile float rod without adding to its weight. To provide greater strength under stress, many manufacturers wrap their carbon blanks in a fine-weave mesh of Kevlar, a material first developed by Du Pont and used in the manufacture of crash helmets and boat hulls.

The rod must feel comfortable beneath your forearm, with either a full cork or a cork/duplon-mix grip, and this brings me to the subject of handle length. While certain manufacturers still insist on over-long handles, resulting in up to 1 ft of the rod (in effective length) protruding behind your elbow and getting in the way, others produce an ideal length of between 22 and 23 in. I have a pet hate, also, against handles that are too thick and thus restrict fluent manipulations of the reel, the ideal diameter being somewhere between 7/8 and 1 in.

Rod rings should be stand-off to eliminate 'line stick' in wet weather, and they should be lined with either silicon carbide or aluminium oxide centres to alleviate unnecessary wear on fine lines. If you intend using a centre-pin reel, ensure there are two rings on the bottom joint between handle and spigot so that the thumb and forefinger of your free hand can easily draw line off for casting.

Poles

There is absolutely no question whatsoever that when it comes to exact bait presentation beneath a float at distances of up to 40 ft out in still or running water (barring gale

Whether pumping the float way out into a windswept gravel pit or flicking it underhand into a sumptuous mill-pool, most situations are covered by a lightweight, 13 ft carbon waggler rod.

force winds), the pole is without equal. These facts were certainly brought home to me over 30 years ago when roach and dace fishing on the rivers Lea and Thames, presenting cubes of bread crust laid on the bottom or trotting casters over loose-fed hempseed. And in those days, prior to the use of carbon fibre in fishing rod construction, poles or 'roach poles' as they were affectionately called then, weighed a ton. Arm or backache, or both, following a lengthy session supporting up to 20 ft of brass-jointed bamboo, were commonplace, but because bait presentation was so superior, with the float immediately beneath the pole tip, no-one complained.

Indeed, I have fond teenage recollections of travelling from north London (where I then lived) with the local club by coach on monthly outings to the drains of Cambridgeshire, where the bamboo roach pole was regularly put to good effect. My favourite venue was the Old Bedford River at Mepal where, in summer, prime rudd up to close on 2 lb could only be winkled out from tiny holes in the thick covering of yellow lilies with the roach pole.

Today, not only are poles longer, lighter and thus more pleasant to use, but due to the European 'elasticated tip', which acts as a built-in shock absorber to a fish pulling hard, much smaller and lighter terminal tackle can be used, compared to the running-line set-up of a float rod. The only disadvantage as far as top-line, reinforced carbon-

With minimum line between tip and float, match fishermen know full well that for superior control up to distances of 10 to 11 m, there is nothing to compare with the effectiveness of the pole, whether you buy a fibreglass telescopic cheaply, or invest in a top-line, reinforced carbon special.

fibre poles are concerned is expense. As you can easily invest as much, if not rather more, than the cost of a roadworthy car in a pole, choosing a suitable one should not be done with haste. Consider all the various options at your local tackle shop (by handling them as though fishing), and go for as light and as rigid a reinforced carbon take-apart pole as you can afford.

While poles up to 14½ m (an incredible 47½ ft) are currently available (and no doubt the advance of match fishing technology will create even longer models), for most pleasure fishing a length of somewhere between 8 and 11 m should suffice.

You have the option of tying the line directly to the tip (flick-tip) of the pole, or cutting the tip back carefully using a fine-tooth hacksaw and adding a PTFE bush, through which runs high-stretch pole elastic. No. 4 elastic is perfect (see Pole fishing, p. 109–10).

Top-of-the-range carbon poles come supplied with a 'top-two kit' – a duplicate of the top two joints (usually telescopic) – enabling one to be used as a flick-tip, the other cut back and elasticated. Also available from some manufacturers is a duplicate top-four or five section kit, allowing you to have at the ready (for a speedy change-over) a complete second, lighter or heavier float rig. You simply change the entire end of the pole at the fourth or fifth joint, and instantly start fishing with a different rig.

Much in vogue for catching smaller species at close range, which makes them particularly suitable for roach, rudd and dace, are the slim-line, super-lightweight carbon 'whips'. These fabulous tools are easily supported beneath the forearm just like a float rod, up to lengths of 6 m. Most are fitted with super-fine carbon flick-tips, onto which a tiny ring is glued. Except for the bottom two joints, whips are telescopic.

Having said all this, and taking into account the relative cost of top-quality carbon poles, you can still quite happily catch roach, rudd and dace at close range with a pole at a fraction of the cost, simply by purchasing an inexpensive hollow-glass telescopic model of 5 to 6 m. These 'cheapies' usually incorporate a solid-glass tip, to which you whip a loop of thick mono (20 lb test) or glue on a mini tip-ring. Telescopic poles up to 6 m can be held for quite some time supported by the forearm without undue fatigue, and while they are rather sloppy in action, this does act as a buffer when you hook into a 1 lb roach on a size 20 hook tied to a 1 lb test bottom. They are equally good for bullying larger roach and rudd hooked amongst heavy weed or lilies on lines of 2 and 3 lb test with hooks tied direct.

Ledger rods

When considering ledger rods for small species like roach, rudd and dace, there are three pointers worth bearing in mind: length, power, or rather sensitivity, and whether to opt for a model with a threaded tip-ring into which a swingtip, springtip or a quivertip (see Bite indicators, p. 60) can be screwed, or a built-in quivertip ledger rod. You could get both if you can afford it. Most quality, slim-profile ledger rods are now made from lightweight carbon fibre, which can be held all day long without fatigue. This allows you to hit more bites successfully while enjoying maximum pleasure from playing even small fish.

For narrow fisheries, streams, canals and so on – in fact, all close-range work when a vast length of line is not going to be pulled through the water in order to ensure the hook is driven home – a 9 or 10 ft rod with a snappy, yet all-through action and a threaded end-ring to accept bite-indicator tips will do the job nicely.

Moving up the scale a little and thinking in terms of placing the bait (together with perhaps a medium-sized swimfeeder) distances of, say, up to 30 yd in both still and flowing water, necessitating a 3 lb reel line, I suggest a slightly longer rod (10–11 ft), again with a snappy action, which, under full compression, also bends into an all-through curve. This helps cushion the strike required (for line pick-up), yet stops small hooks from ripping out or fine hook links from snapping, while permitting the utmost enjoyment from playing even modest-sized roach or rudd, and even dace.

In this medium-range bracket I would suggest a built-in quivertip model or a multi-tip, most of which come complete with two or three extra tips (stored in the handle) of varying sensitivity, so that you can change tips quickly to suit different current strengths.

Lastly, and if much of your ledgering happens to be either at distance into deep, still water, or in exceedingly deep and fast rivers like the Severn, Norfolk's tidal River Yare, or in the lower reaches of the River Bann in Northern Ireland, necessitating feeders of up to 2 oz and a reel line of 4 to 5 lb, then choose the horse for the course – an 11 to 12-footer with a medium-action, built-in quivertip. Many of these powerful models are referred to as Avon quivertips, and possess enough meat in the lower two-thirds to combat the fast water of rivers like the Hampshire Avon, coupled with a surprising degree of sensitivity. in the finely tapered quivertip, permitting bite detection from the shyest roach.

The Avon twin-tip ledger, which incorporates both standard (with a threaded end-ring) and built-in quivertip tops, is the ideal outfit if you regularly concentrate upon both fast rivers and big stillwaters, where versatility and a touch of power is required. The standard tip, for instance, may be employed without a tip indicator, when distance ledgering for specimen stillwater rudd and roach, and a bobbin bite indicator fixed on the line between butt ring and reel is much preferred.

As with float rods, insist on a narrow cork handle of between ⅞ and 1 in diameter, and no longer than 21–22 in, otherwise it will feel awkward and inhibit you from holding it when you should be – thus causing you to miss shy bites.

A standard 9–10 ft ledger rod incorporating a screw-in tip-ring that accommodates both swing and quivertip bite indicators, will cover most situations from the smallest stream to a large, open stillwater, where Bob Nudd hooked this fine roach.

Fly rods

To obtain the utmost pleasure from catching dace and roach on the fly from overgrown streams and small rivers, I scale right down to a 7½ ft carbon brook rod that takes a size 4 or 5 line. For larger rivers and stillwaters where the occasional long cast might just be needed in order to reach those awkward sanctuary habitats beside reedbeds or beneath the branches of overhanging trees, a 9-footer that throws a 5 or 6 line will prove a better tool. Harsh, reservoir-style rods are definitely out if you wish to obtain the best action from coarse species on artificials.

Because it provides direct contact between drum and float tip, the most effective reel for long trotting is the centre-pin. John has fitted a line guard, enabling him to take specimen roach like this beauty pushing 2½ lb, at distances of up to 30 yd from his local River Wensum.

REELS

Centre-pin reels

There is nothing to match the sensitivity and direct contact between hooked fish and your thumb gently putting pressure on the rim of the drum that is provided by the centre-pin reel. This is why I prefer to use the centre-pin reel when floatfishing for all small to medium–sized species at close range in stillwaters and, of course, for long trotting where the initial cast is no further than, say, three rod

For both ledgering and floatfishing, a compact, fixed-spool reel that runs smoothly on ball-bearings and is fitted with a super-sensitive slipping clutch is imperative when using fine lines, especially when hoping to catch roach such as this one without a breakage.

lengths. I have in current use two favourite and exceptionally free-running centre-pins; the Adcock Stanton and the narrow-drum match aerial. Neither are cheap. They cost rather more than the equivalent in a top-quality fixed-spool reel, but each gives a lifetime of pleasure.

The secret of the centre-pin is its simple design. Because the thumb releases pressure on the drum for line to be given instantly with the minimum of torque on fine lines and tiny hooks (compared to the roller or pin around which the line travels at right angles on closed-face and fixed-spool reels), the centre pin is technically by far the best reel to use at close range. Beyond distances of, say, 15 yd, the fixed-spool reel covers all my requirements for both floatfishing and ledgering.

Fixed-spool reels

To catch smaller species of freshwater fish, I find that a lightweight, small-format fixed-spool provides the greatest pleasure. It should incorporate a roller in the bale arm to help minimize friction against fine lines, and run smoothly on ball-bearings. Models that come complete with two spools allow for a choice of 2 to 2½ lb test on one to cover most floatfishing, and on the other, 3 to 4 and even 5 lb test (depending on the circumstances) for ledgering. The spools of most top-quality reels, such as those manufactured by Shimano, Daiwa, Ryobi, and so on, are now purposely designed to take just 100 yd of line without the need for unwanted and wasteful backing beneath.

The ideal size is between 1,000 and 2,500 – certainly no larger. Reels of a heavier, larger format are less complementary to fine lines in that the slipping clutch is invariably less sensitive. And if you play fish by adjusting and using the clutch for the purpose for which it was invented (as opposed to backwinding), a smooth, super-sensitive clutch that reacts to small increases of pressure from the drag knob, one digit at a time, is imperative.

I have been referring here, of course, to modern stern-drag skirted-spool reels, because the miniature reels of yesteryear, such as the famous baby Mitchel 308 and 408 models (snap one of these up secondhand if you get the chance) were blessed with incredibly sensitive, front-adjusting clutches – absolutely ideal for the fine lines associated with catching the smaller species. I am even tempted to suggest that few reels today are fitted with such effective clutch systems, but this would not be strictly true, because many of the small-format, stern-drag, fixed-spool reels on the market (and I stress small format) do possess smooth slipping clutches. It is well worth mastering the use of the drag knob so that line is taken only at a certain pre-set pressure. It results in one of the most enjoyable parts of playing a fish.

Fly reels

As long-distance casting is not necessary when fly-fishing for coarse species, all that is needed is a simple, rim-control, single-action reel with a ratchet. While being light and reasonably small, there should be room for sufficient backing so the fly line completely fills the spool. The line will then possess minimal 'memory', and will pull from the reel in large, limp coils.

To take size 4 and 5 lines, the Leeda mini 50 fly reel and the Ryobi MG 250S magnesium are ideal, while size 6 lines are perfectly matched to the Leeda lightweight 60, and Ryobi MG 355S magnesium.

Lines

While match fishermen seem perfectly happy about using lines down to 1½ lb test on the reel, I am not. I prefer a greater margin of safety against breakage (and the possibility of harm to wildlife) between the terminal rig and the rod, considering the amount of wear monofilament suffers as it is continually pulled back and forwards through rod rings, often under severe pressure. Besides, only at the hook end does the diameter make any significant difference between bites and no bites. So I never fish with less than a 2 lb reel line.

For long trotting in fast currents where a really large roach may be on the cards, then a 2½ lb test again offers an increased degree of safety. Brands I can recommend for their reliability (for float and ledger fishing) are Sylcast,

Bayer Perlon and Maxima. Maxima is particularly useful for waggler fishing in stillwater because it sinks much more easily than other brands. Incidentally, to ensure any monofilament line sinks quickly, dab a drop of neat washing-up liquid around the spool every so often.

For most close-range ledgering, I find 3 lb test a fine all-round choice, even when casting small feeders. But for swimfeeder ledgering into fast and deep, or distant swims, a 4 lb test reel line again provides that valuable safety margin, especially when a big bream or a barbel might just happen along in between roach bites.

Never forget that the elasticity in monofilament is the safeguard against ripping out small hooks or snapping fine hook lengths on the strike. Only if long-distance trotting or ledgering would I contemplate using low-stretch mono on the reel. As hook lengths, low diameter and low stretch monofilament has much to offer, and I suggest a selection of spools in tests from 12 oz to 1½ lb is an invaluable addition to your tackle-box. Brands like Drennan Double Strength or Aikens Concept 2000 are particularly recommended. Their reduced diameter, compared to standard, 'stretchy' monofilament, creates far less water resistance, allowing the bait to behave more naturally and encouraging more bites. When pole fishing with an elasticated tip, hook lengths down to 8 oz can be used with confidence due to the in-built buffer. With the flick-tip, on the other hand, it would be wise to stick to standard 'stretchy' brands.

HOOKS

Roach, rudd and dace may be considered small, but there are occasions, when seeking specimen roach and rudd in particular, when an 8 or even a size 6 hook is none too large. At the opposite end of the scale, extremely clear or cold water conditions could dictate the use of ridiculously small hooks before roach and dace will bite. I stop at a size 22 tied to a low-diameter, 12 oz hook length. If I became involved in competition fishing on really hard venues like over-fished canals, then no doubt, in order to instigate bites, I would contemplate the use of tiny size 24 and 26 hooks tied to gossamer-thin, 8 oz bottoms.

Steve Allen of Norwich gently slips a size 18 spade-end hook tied to a 1½ lb hook length from the lips of a superbly conditioned, winter river roach. In clear, cold-water conditions, there are times when, unless you step down to light tackle, bites simply do not happen.

The choice between spade-end and eyed hooks is quite clear. Using size 12 hooks and larger, when bigger baits such as bread flake are liable to cover the entire hook, and the neatness of the knot is inconsequential, I use the Drennan, chemically-etched, round-bend, straight-eyed, carbon specimen hook, which is strongly forged yet lightweight. In sizes 14 to 22 I use spade-ends exclusively, and the choice of pattern depends on several factors. With large baits such as stewed wheat, sweetcorn and bread crust presented on a size 14 or even a 16, if big roach or rudd are the quarry and the hook is tied direct to, for example, a 2 lb reel line, I prefer a forged spade-end, such as Kamasan B640 or a Mustad 495. Conversely, for a size 14 or 16 tied to a 1½ lb bottom for presenting punched bread, casters or an elderberry to shy dace or roach, I choose lighter, fine-wire patterns, such as the micro-barb Kamasan B520 and B620 or Drennan carbon match hooks.

Strength of hook lengths or reel lines (when tied direct) must at all times be compatible with the hook pattern – a factor many anglers totally ignore and one that is responsible for more lost fish than any other single reason. So do not tie an extra-fine wire, unforged 22 direct to a 2 lb reel line and expect it not to straighten with a lively 1½ lb rudd pulling on the line. If quality fish are expected, and they will only accept small baits on small hooks, use a small, forged hook such as a Mustad 39862 or Kamasan B920 and step down to a 1½ lb hook length – thus creating a balanced end-rig.

KNOTS

For tying spade-end hooks to the finest monofilament, it is worth learning to tie the simple knot in fig. 5A, which requires no threading or special tool, and allows you to tie the smallest of hooks direct to the reel line or a lighter hook length or bottom quickly. It really is easy. If your fingers and eyesight will not co-operate, however, there are several excellent tools for tying on spade-end hooks, such as the matchman hooktyer.

For tying on eyed hooks I use one of two knots. With large hooks, where the line can be passed twice through the eye, the mahseer knot in fig. 5B is unbeatable. In the smaller sizes of chemically etched, eyed hooks, however, the eye is usually so small that the line will pass through only once, and so I use the seven-turn, tucked half blood knot in fig. 5C.

For joining a fine hook length (or bottom) to the reel line, or for constructing a simple, fixed-paternoster ledger rig, the four-turn water knot in fig. 6A is superb. This easy, neat and completely reliable knot also allows you to join a much lighter hook length to the reel line, as in fig. 6B, or to add a thicker ledger or feeder link to the reel line, which helps alleviate tangles, as in fig. 6C.

By now it will be plainly obvious that running ledger rigs play absolutely no part in my fishing. They are, in fact, unnecessary and no more sensitive to a biting fish than the simple fixed paternoster, which, owing to the neat junction knot, creates minimal resistance and attracts

nowhere near so much weed and bottom debris as swivels,
booms and anti-tangle rigs.

The last knot I suggest you learn to tie – the simple
sliding stop knot – is shown in fig. 6D. This is tied directly
on to the reel line (using a 10 in length of the same) above a
sliding float, which rises and locks at the depth at which
the knot is tied. Remember not to trim the ends of the line
too short. Around 1 in is a good length, so the ends fold
when passing through the rod rings.

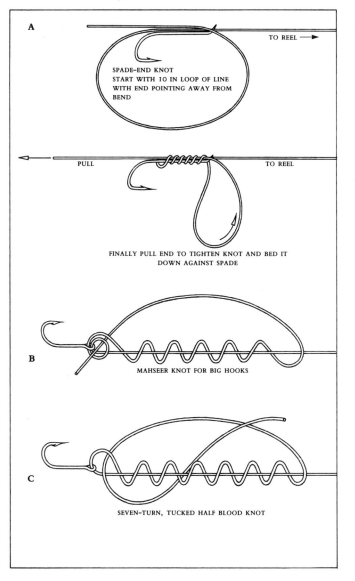

FIGURE 5 *Knots 1*

A

TO REEL →

SPADE-END KNOT
START WITH 10 IN LOOP OF LINE
WITH END POINTING AWAY FROM
BEND

← PULL   TO REEL

FINALLY PULL END TO TIGHTEN KNOT AND BED IT
DOWN AGAINST SPADE

B

MAHSEER KNOT FOR BIG HOOKS

C

SEVEN-TURN, TUCKED HALF BLOOD KNOT

FIGURE 6 *Knots 2*

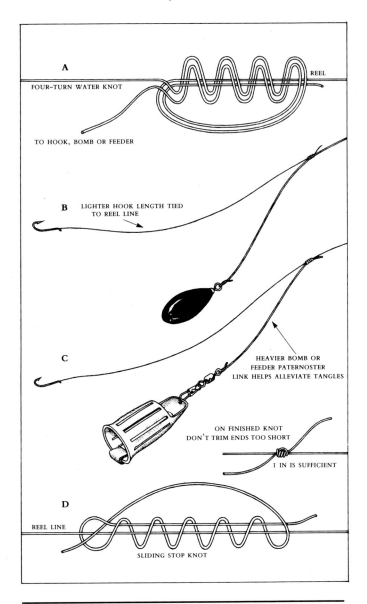

A

FOUR-TURN WATER KNOT   REEL

TO HOOK, BOMB OR FEEDER

B   LIGHTER HOOK LENGTH TIED
     TO REEL LINE

C

HEAVIER BOMB OR
FEEDER PATERNOSTER
LINK HELPS ALLEVIATE TANGLES

ON FINISHED KNOT
DON'T TRIM ENDS TOO SHORT

I IN IS SUFFICIENT

D

REEL LINE

SLIDING STOP KNOT

FLOATS

Attached to the ceiling of my tackle shop is a long, vertical display of float cards containing well over 100 different sizes, lengths and shapes of modern floats. What perhaps complicates the choice even more is the fact that there is not a float on show that I could not use for catching roach, rudd and dace, given the right circumstances.

In order to present the bait to a 6 in roach inhabiting an

Martin Founds caught
this superb rudd from
Denmark's River
Guden, and to hook
rudd or roach in a fast-
flowing river you need
to be really certain
about two things –
that your hook is
strongly forged and the
knot you tie it with is
sound. See Hooks and
Knots.

overgrown canal or farm pond, a sensitive antenna like a
small stillwater green carrying just two No. 1 shots is quite
sufficient. Conversely, to catch that same 6-in roach from
the fast, deep waters of the River Severn or a large,
windswept lake where you need to fish at distance, a
bodied or loaded waggler carrying up to the equivalent of
three swan shots is needed.

I am not suggesting that you need to become a walking
tackle shop, but you should relate your float choice to the
venues and conditions at hand, stocking up with the
patterns most suited to where you fish. Let me therefore
relate float selection to some of the venues and conditions
mentioned in the chapter on location, starting with
diminutive fisheries.

For presenting small
baits like maggots and
casters at close range
in running water, the
stick float reigns
supreme. Held back
hard, as shown here,
it encourages the bait
to swing attractively
upwards ahead of the
float, which is fixed
top and bottom with
silicon tubing.

Stillwater floats

For delicate bait presentation in ponds, small lakes and canals you require a range of fine-tipped antennas in shotting capacities from two No. 1s up to 3AA, plus a range of loaded antennas, or darts, for fishing ultra-light and on the drop in sizes two No. 4s to 2BB.

For fishing further out into gravel pits, estate lakes and even larger stillwaters, such as reservoirs and Irish loughs, the most useful float is the waggler. A range each of plain straight, tipped and bodied wagglers in sizes from 2BB up to 3 swans is indispensible and exceptionally versatile because you will also need these in flowing water. In addition, for distance fishing on stillwaters, a range of loaded wagglers (almost self-cocking) that take minimal shot down the line, permit extremely sensitive presentation for both on-the-bottom and on-the-drop techniques.

River floats

In addition to the three types of wagglers previously mentioned, I would suggest a series of trotting floats that are attached with silicon tubing at the top and bottom. At the lighter end, wire-stem stick floats carrying from three No. 8 up to 3BB are superb for easing the bait through at close range in slow currents. I would also suggest at least one heavier pattern, such as a range of big sticks or balsa trotters carrying from around 3BB up to 3½AA.

For currents demanding still more shots to get the bait down and keep it there – weir-pool fishing and the like – a range of chunky-bodied, Avon-style floats carrying from 3 to 6AA, or the lighter Haskins cork on crowquill specials, are just the job.

Plain peacock quill

I would also recommend that you carry in your kit a few stems of plain, unpainted peacock quill of varying thickness, for stret pegging and for presenting a flat float when surface fishing for rudd and dace (see Techniques and Rigs, pp. 121 and 104).

POLE FLOATS AND RIGS

Nowadays the range of pole floats available is almost as comprehensive as running-line patterns. Indeed, from the European and British match-fishing scene entire new ranges of pole floats are born each season. Do not be misled into thinking that unless your float-box contains the latest in modern design, you will not catch. Roach, rudd and dace are adequately covered by just five basic patterns. These, like all pole floats, are attached by threading the line through a tiny ring on the top of the body and at the bottom of the stem with a fine piece of silicon tubing.

Many pole floats have bodies based on an elongated heart shape. Those constructed with the wide end uppermost are more suitable for flowing water. Conversely, if the body is positioned upside down with the narrow part at the top, it is ideal for still or very slow-moving water because it creates less resistance to a biting fish.

Stillwater floats

For the most delicate, close-range, fine-line presentation in small waters, a slim-bodied, bristle-top range taking from three to six No. 12 shots is perfect. Going up in size, the next range should have a slim, reversed body with a shotting capacity from 0.05 g up to 0.30 g – perfect for presentation with the whip or with a long pole and short line.

For greater stability in still water, when you want a shotting capacity of between 0.25 g and 1.50 g, again choose a reversed heart or oval body with a slightly thicker tip so it can be seen easily at distances up to 10–12 m, even in a good ripple.

River patterns

I would suggest a round or heart-shaped, bodied wire-stem range with a shotting capacity of between 0.30 g and 1.50 g, plus a much heavier set taking from 2 up to 7 or

A match in progress along the tidal reaches of the River Wensum in the heart of Norwich, and to the man, every competitor is offering the bait directly beneath a long carbon-fibre pole. With the water clear and the roach decidedly shy, hooks are tied to a 1 lb hook length and used in conjunction with an elasticated pole-tip.

even 8 g. These bulbous patterns may look cumbersome and insensitive, but for holding back hard in order to ease the bait slowly along the river-bed in low water temperatures during the winter months, and for the best presentation in strong currents, you do need a good-sized, buoyant body. As long as it is shotted right down so that only the float tip is visible above the surface until you start to hold back, even the largest-bodied pole floats provide sensitive and natural presentation of the bait.

For shotting these larger floats easily, invest in a comprehensive selection of olivette weights from 1 up to 8 g. Being hollow, they are easily threaded onto the line and stopped 2–3 ft from the hook by a small shot, so your bait goes straight down to where it needs to be. It is then a simple case of adding just one or two small shots between the olivette and the hook to balance the rig.

Contrary to popular belief, it is not obligatory to own an entire boxful of pole rigs ready made-up on plastic winders, to cover every eventuality in both still and running water. The speed factor demanded by match fishing is, of course, responsible for this idea. It is comforting, however, especially when fingers are numb or the light is poor, to have a small selection of made-up rigs suitable for the fishing at hand. Remember to purchase plastic winders wide and long enough to accommodate the more portly, bulbous patterns of river floats.

When you are using tiny hooks, instead of tying on a new bottom or a hook length of fine mono plus a new hook every time a breakage occurs, followed by a re-adjustment of the shots, it makes sense to use hooks-to-nylon. As all come tied to bottoms of identical length, a quick 'loop to loop' change-over soon has you fishing again with little more than a small shot or two to adjust.

POLE TIPS

Flicktip fishing is best when using light tackle on a whip-style pole, or when presenting reasonably large hooks and baits (such as a bunch of maggots or a grain of wheat on a size 12) tied direct to 2 lb line. In other words, in the case of the whip, the safety margin, or buffer, lies in its fine, flexible tip, or with heavier lines tied direct to the top ring of telescopic glass or rigid carbon poles. However, when sensitive bait presentation to spooky fish in clear or cold water demands the use of gossamer-fine hook lengths, down to 12 oz or less, and size 22 hooks, a 'buffer' needs to be added to the rig or one of two things will happen. Either fish will repeatedly bounce off on the strike, or, worse still, you will instantly break off whenever a reasonably good fish grabs hold. And this is where the elasticated pole tip comes in.

As can be seen from fig. 7, it is not difficult to convert the top section or top two sections of a long, rigid pole using one of the many kits available. Cut the tip back carefully a little at a time with a fine-toothed, junior hacksaw so that the hollow PTFE bush fits in neatly, and smooth the edges with emery cloth. The connector to which the end loop of the made-up rig is tied will fit inside the bush, but you first need to tie on the elastic supplied with the made-up rig (ideally you need size 3 or 4) and thread it down through the tip.

Fit the coned 'uni bung' to which the other end of the elastic is tied into the opposite (wider) end of the joint (see fig. 7). To ensure that it slides several inches up into the joint, you can cut off the plastic uni bung at its wide end to reduce its diameter. When you have finished elasticating the pole tip, a thin plastic tail (connected to the uni bung)

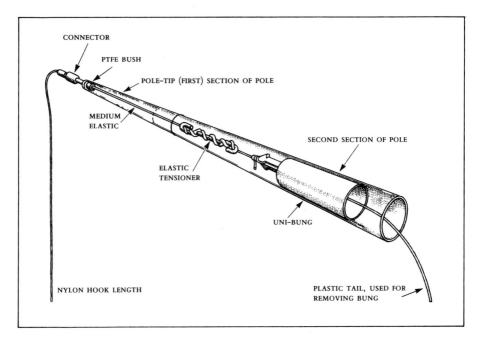

CONNECTOR

PTFE BUSH

POLE-TIP (FIRST) SECTION OF POLE

MEDIUM
ELASTIC

SECOND SECTION OF POLE

ELASTIC
TENSIONER

UNI-BUNG

NYLON HOOK LENGTH

PLASTIC TAIL, USED FOR
REMOVING BUNG

FIGURE 7 *Pole tip elastic conversion – using standard pole elastic kit*

should protrude from the joint. This you pull gently to remove the bung to facilitate a change of elastic. As a precaution against abrasion, which can reduce the effective life of the elastic, add a few drops of special lubricant. The elastic will then stretch effortlessly, allowing you to land the very largest roach or rudd on the tiniest hook.

BITE INDICATORS

Swingtip

For the most sensitive bite indication when ledgering in still and very slow-moving water, choose a lightweight fibreglass swingtip of between 10 and 12 in. Just like floats, swingtips have coloured ends, so select one you can see clearly against a variety of backgrounds. Ensure that the threaded silicone junction that screws into the tip-ring of your ledger rod is flexible but not floppy, and that the end ring at the tip is good quality and not liable to shred fine lines. A loaded (weighted) swingtip is required for slow-moving rivers, and when this starts lifting to current pressure against the line, change the swing for a quivertip.

A target board placed immediately behind the swingtip (once the tackle has been cast and the rod placed on rod-rests) will allow you to see the tiniest of tip movements. Target boards are also useful when watching quivertips in low water temperatures, when bites are liable to be tiny movements of between $\frac{1}{8}$ to $\frac{1}{4}$ in. You can easily make your own target boards or invest in one of the many commercial models available. Either way, it should be reversible (so the tip can be angled to the left or to the right) and accept the standard bankstick thread.

Quivertips

The choice of quivertips, in both carbon fibre and solid fibreglass, is almost as comprehensive as that of ledgering rods. By far the most versatile bite indicator, the quivertip is available in a whole range of test curves from 1 to $3\frac{1}{2}$ oz to suit current strengths from the slow draw on a canal, to a fast, deep run on the lower reaches of a tidal river where a 2 oz feeder is needed to hold bottom.

My preference for tip colour is all-white. This I can see easily against any background. Indeed, all my built-in quivertip rods have the top 16–20 in painted in two coats of matt white. A white tip is great when, if like me, you prefer to illuminate it for night fishing with a narrow torch beam (see Quivertipping for specimens at night, p. 96).

Screw-in, commercially-made quivertips, most of which have just a single ring at the tip, are best doctored by adding a small intermediate guide midway along so that the line is fully supported and follows the contour of the tip when it is under maximum compression.

When purchasing powerful 3 to $3\frac{1}{2}$ oz test curve quivertips for deep and fast waters, ensure that the tip is not thicker and more powerful than the end of your rod, as modern carbon, lightweight ledger rods are extremely fine at the tip.

Springtips

The springtip is a solid glass, tapered quivertip that passes through the middle of a 2 in long spring into a rubber

*When cold water
conditions mean that
bites may register as
mere 'trembles', they
are much easier to see
if you watch the rod
tip against the lines of
a target board,
whether using a
swingtip, a springtip
or a quivertip bite
indicator.*

moulding with a tip-ring thread. It can, in effect, be used as a fairly stiff quivertip. Or it can be used by pulling gently on the tip so that it leaves the spring but remains in the rubber joint, like a springtip that hinges at the junction. Used like this it creates far less resistance to biting fish than the quivertip, and in still or slow-moving water is ideal for small fish like roach and dace.

As with commercially-made quivertips, which come fitted with just the end ring, it is worth doctoring springtips by whipping on a small guide midway between thread and tip-ring.

Bobbin indicators

Bobbin bite indicators, which clip onto the line between the reel and the butt ring and are retained by a cord fixed to the front rod-rest, may have limited appeal, but they are nevertheless extremely useful in certain circumstances. I much prefer them for stillwater ledgering, especially at distance, when using large baits intended for specimen rudd and roach, when generally a strike would only be made at positive indications.

Daytime bobbins, which come complete with clip and retaining cord, such as the tenpin bobbin, are available in

When presenting the bait in fast currents during the winter months, there is no finer indicator for ledgering than the quivertip. John uses an 11 ft, Avon-style, built-in quivertip ledger rod for most of his winter roach fishing. This splendid specimen fell for a ¼ in cube of bread crust ledgered static in a deep weir-pool.

fluorescent red. The glo bobbin, which contains a luminous betalight element that lasts for 15 years, provides indication around the clock.

To counteract 'bobbin lift' in strong winds wherever there is a strong draw or sub-surface tow on stillwaters, simply pinch between one and three swan shots on the retaining cord immediately below the bobbin.

Electronic bite indicators

Used in conjunction with clip-on bobbins for long sessions when you are searching for specimen rudd and roach inhabiting large stillwaters like reservoirs and estate lakes, electronic gadgetry is totally justified and a real boon. When few bites are expected because there are not many fish, there is no point in concentrating on the bobbins (assuming a two-rod set-up is employed) for hour upon hour. Much better to relax and enjoy the surroundings and natural history and to be ready for striking when a bite does occur.

The most efficient unit is the standard, cordless Optonic, which screws into a standard bankstick to become the front rod-rest and which is available in either a low- or a high-bleep tone.

SUNDRIES

Bread punch

Of the numerous designs of bread-punch units available, I much prefer the pen type, such as the Seymo bread punch, which comes with four interchangeable brass heads, or the plastic Drennan bread punches. The latter consists of a set of four plastic punches with heads varying from 2 mm up to 5 mm in diameter, suitable for hooks in sizes 10 to 24. What I most like about these is the extra-shallow bowls, which really compress thick-sliced bread but only lightly compress thin slices – a feature that allows you to control the rate at which your bait descends through the swim.

Drennan punches are shanfered below the slot, so that when the hook is pulled through into the bread pellet and out, the point is not blunted by the bowl.

Disgorgers

To remove a hook safely from any fish, whether a 3 in dace that has completely swallowed a size 22 hook, or a specimen rudd that needs a size 8, eyed hook eased gently from its throat, you need to be equipped with two items of tackle. A pair of long-nosed artery forceps between 5 and 8 in long, and a barrel-type plastic or alloy disgorger.

Roach, rudd and dace are delicate species, so be exceptionally careful of their throat tissue during hook removal. Always hold them firmly, but gently, with wet hands so as not to remove their protective mucus or slime, and refrain from any heavy prodding with the disgorger. Whenever a hook proves impossible to dislodge, cut the line and allow the fish to rid itself of the alien object. Hooks almost fall out by themselves when the fish is released and its muscles become relaxed again.

Bait-droppers and catapults

To keep shoal fish feeding confidently, the accurate delivery of loose feed and groundbait is of paramount importance. Bait-droppers that attach to the hook and deposit particle feed such as maggots, casters and hempseed straight down to the bottom, exactly where you want it in fast deep rivers, or both, are indispensible.

Wire-mesh models cost double the price of plastic droppers, but are far more durable and have in-built weight for a speedy descent to the bottom. The secret in using droppers is smoothness of operation, because if they are suddenly jerked while they are sinking, they may open prematurely and the bait will not come to rest anywhere near its intended destination. Consequently, never actually cast the dropper. Swing it out slowly on the end of a long line and retrieve it only when the leaded trigger arm touches bottom and the dropper deposits its load.

Because the accurate use of bait-droppers is obviously restricted to swims that are little further than one and a half rod lengths out, all distances beyond this should be covered by the catapult. You require two models: a medium-sized, soft pouch catapult with stretchy elastic for putting out maggots, hempseed, sweetcorn, and so on; and another with a larger, rigid pouch and more powerful elastic for propelling tangerine-sized balls of groundbait beyond throwing distance.

Bait, whether loose feed or balls of stodge, holds together much better if your movements are progressive and steady. The shock of a quick pullback followed by a sudden, violent release is quite liable to make balls of cereal disintegrate – and maggots scatter all over the place, attracting fish to every spot except the desired one. It is fair to say that unless you work at catapulting accurately, you could find that it has a detrimental effect on your sport.

Feeding fish naturally follow the food source just as quickly away from the desired area as they moved to it. So be very careful during those first few pouchfuls of loose feed. During windy conditions, especially, practise with just a couple of maggots or casters in the pouch instead of unintentionally freebaiting the wrong line.

Landing-nets

As even the largest roach or rudd is unlikely to exceed 16 or 17 in in length (even a 2 lb roach will only measure

Roach, rudd and dace have extremely soft, sensitive throat tissue, and by far the best tool for the removal of tiny hooks is a barrel disgorger. For large-eyed hooks, use long-nosed artery forceps.

Fish quickly respond to an introduced food source, and can as easily move away from the area in which your bait lies as they can move towards it. Work at being extremely accurate when using the catapult, whether loose feeding or putting out balls of cereal feed.

Terry Smith and Bob Nudd certainly needed a big net for this massive combined catch of stillwater roach. Always invest in the largest keep-net you can afford so that your catch is returned unharmed at the end of the day.

around 14 in) a landing-net top of 18 in diameter is quite sufficient. There are many excellent, extremely lightweight designs on the market with triangle, round, bow and spoon-shaped frames, made from both plastic-covered alloy and solid glass or carbon. The flexiglass nets made by Keenets, for instance, are only half the weight of a normal net. Whatever type you choose, insist on a reasonably shallow, nylon, minnow-mesh net with a fine micro-mesh pan base, which does not allow tiny shots to slip through and become tangled.

Match anglers use even smaller pan nets of just 12 in diameter when expecting only small fish, and in truth, even a 1½ lb roach will not prove troublesome. Much of my own fishing, however, rather contradicts this line of thought. In my local rivers Wensum and Bure, where roach are not uncommon over the 2½ lb mark, I may also catch chub over 4 lb, or the odd big bream or even a double-figure barbel, while roach fishing. So I hedge my bets by using a 24-in diameter round net, which engulfs them all. It is rather on the large side for most of the roach I catch, but not for specimen roach and rudd caught after dark, when netting is far from easy.

With regard to landing-net poles, I would suggest you purchase the longest and lightest model, in lightweight hollow glass, that you can afford. Telescopic models of up to 10 ft in carbon fibre are first class. There is nothing more frustrating than not being able to net a fish caught up in the fringe of marginal vegetation because the landing-net pole is too short, or because you cannot hold it when fully extended because with the net-top it is too heavy.

To weigh a specimen roach, rudd or dace, unscrew the net-top and hoist it onto the hook of the scales, remembering to deduct the weight of the net afterwards. Transferring the fish to a 'designer' weigh-bag or sling only creates extra stress on the fish.

Keep-nets

By far the kindest keep-net material is soft, black, nylon micro-mesh. Whether you choose round or square rings is not important, although rectangular nets have greater stability in shallow water and in windy weather. What is of paramount importance, however, is that you purchase the largest keep-net you can afford, because roach, rudd and dace are extremely delicate species and quickly suffer from stress when crammed into small nets or nets with considerably larger meshes, through which their fins can poke and easily become split.

Wonderful keep-nets are available with built-in, angle-lock top rings in a rectangular format with 20 x 16 in rings, up to 13 ft in length, and round nets in both 18 in and 21 in diameter rings up to 11½ ft in length. My overall preference is for a round, 21 in diameter net, 10 ft in length, preferably with the protector net facility, which allows the entire catch to be released through the bottom of the net (without taking it from the water) by undoing a plastic clip on each side of the bottom ring.

CHAPTER SIX

BAITS

AT the bottom of my garden there is a lake where the depth at the margins drops quickly away to around 12 ft. Throughout the summer months this spot is regularly visited by numbers of tench. Bordered by reedy shallows at each end of the sudden depression, it is part of a patrol route to which they are attracted. I help matters along by introducing a handful or two of peanuts every day.

Now, like carp and chub, once they have acquired a taste for them tench really respond well to peanuts, and strangely enough, so do the large shoals of roach and rudd that frequent this part of the lake. In fact, unless the tench are quick off the mark, most of the loose feed is mopped up by roach in the 6 to 12 oz bracket.

It is probably fair to say that canal fishermen, who consider a single maggot and size 22 hook to be standard roach tackle, would be flabbergasted at the thought of an 8 oz roach inhaling a jumbo-sized American peanut on an 8 hook tied direct to 4 lb line (tench fishing, remember) but roach and rudd adore peanuts.

This example illustrates the importance of pre-baiting if your object is to wean fish on to a new bait, so that they bite with more confidence, or to attract the shoal to a particular area. I hope it also makes you think beyond using simply maggots when in pursuit of these three species, because it is difficult to think of any bait (apart from live or dead fish) that in the right circumstances will not be taken by roach, rudd and dace.

NATURAL BAITS

Caddis grubs

Long before I purchased maggots, or 'gentils' as they were popularly called in those days, my hook baits were gathered from wherever I happened to be fishing. There

As maggots are so readily accessible, most anglers would not dream of collecting caddis grubs nowadays, as John used to do in his youth. Nonetheless, they are a superb and entirely free source of bait that is always available at the waterside. So if you forget the maggot box . . . !

are, in fact, over 200 different species of sedge or caddis flies inhabiting both still and running water, and it is their larvae, known affectionately as the 'caddis grub', which roach, rudd and dace (along with most other freshwater species) consume with relish. Most species of caddis construct intricate little homes of between 1 and 2 in long from pieces of wood, stone or sand, which act both as house and protection for one year, from the moment when the grub emerges from the egg laid by the sedge fly until the grub leaves its home. Once the pupa moves towards the surface in readiness for the last stage of metamorphosis, its body case eventually splits open and out crawls the sedge fly itself. It is a fascinating life cycle.

To gather a fresh supply of grubs, you simply rummage around in the shallows, lifting up large twigs and rotten branches and looking under large pieces of flint, etc., to which the grubs cling. If you peer intently through crystal-clear water, you can see them crawling awkwardly along the bottom with just their head and legs extended beyond their protective case.

To remove the succulent grub (noticeably larger than a white maggot), pinch its tail end to make the head and legs appear at the front. Then gently ease it out with thumb and forefinger. Present one up on a size 14, or two on a 12, and

Even large worms will catch rudd, roach and dace in the right circumstances. Dace inhabiting overgrown streams and swift-flowing rivers gobble up lobworms greedily, often taking on considerably more than they can chew.

Summer or winter, in slow water, fast water, clear water, cold water, even in flood water, the attraction of the humble maggot never wanes. Maggots are as attractive to 2 in rudd as they are to a 2 lb roach.

you have a superb, entirely free, natural bait that is there whenever you fish, just waiting to be harvested both winter and summer should you forget the maggots, or simply wish to enjoy a piece of natural history.

Worms

Whether procured from the lawn at night with the aid of a torch after heavy rain, or dug from the garden, lobworms make a superb floodwater bait for roach when the river is running fast, tea-coloured and up over the banks. A whole large lob ledgered close in to the bank in a slack is at such times the most selective specimen-roach bait of all. Once the river recedes to normal levels, however, it has been my experience that roach switch off to worms. Dace, though, and again especially large dace, seem willing to chew on a lobworm at almost any time except in really low water temperatures when their metabolic rate and thus their appetite reduce, and they accept only much smaller offerings.

Of the three species, rudd are the most interested in worms, and wherever they live in crowded, overstocked waters, they immediately set on lobworms, brandlings and small redworms with real aggression. I have on numerous occasions, while out winter perch fishing on small lakes and pits using ledgered lobworms during really cold conditions, experienced tentative bites on the bobbin that never seem to develop. And in most cases, by halving the worm and re-casting using only the tail end, a nice bonus rudd has been the result.

Maggots

By far the cheapest and most readily available of all naturals, maggots have become the universal bait for most smaller species. Being small and grub-like in format and not dissimilar to one of the most common underwater naturals, the caddis larvae, small wonder maggots are instantly sucked in, converted to pulp by the pharyngeal teeth and swallowed. At this point, allow me to enlarge upon the problem of 'sucked maggots', which return as mere skins, having been squeezed of their creamy inner juices, because if this happens regularly you are not striking early enough.

If you move the lowest (tell-tale) shot of your float rig closer to the hook or shot the float tip right down until it is a mere blimp on the surface, you will see the bite earlier. Conversely, when ledgering, use a much shorter tail or hook length and strike at the tiniest indication of a bite. Plain, shop-bought maggots, which are bred from the second-most-common European bluebottle (the softer-skinned 'gozzer' maggots come from the most common bluebottle), are easily coloured with non-carcinogenic liquid dyes. Or they can be purchased ready coloured in red, green, yellow, bronze or mixed.

For most situations I place my confidence in a box of plain white maggots well-sieved of debris, to which fresh maize meal has been added to stop them from sweating. During the cold months of winter, however, when the water is particularly clear, with next to no natural vegetation visible, the stark white of a maggot does, I am sure, sometimes inhibit fish in accepting it. I am not talking about stunted rudd in a farm pond or a 500-strong shoal of immature dace crammed into the tail end of a weir race. Neither of these have the opportunity to be selective when they must always compete aggressively for food. However, roach living in a river that, week in and week out, receives the attention of fishermen by the hundreds learn to be suspicious and extremely choosey. And I am sure in such circumstances that a bronze maggot is more readily acceptable – even if in reality it is not. However, because I believe it is more acceptable, I fish with much more confidence, if you fish with confidence you are likely to catch more fish. When seeking small fish in extremely cold, clear water a reduction in maggot size will sometimes produce more confident bites on light float tackle incorporating hooks in sizes 22 and smaller.

This is where either pinkies (the maggot of the green-bottle) or squatts (the maggot of a small house fly) can prove useful. Being lighter, squatts are particularly suited to on-the-drop fishing with an ultra-light terminal rig.

For the most natural presentation, try not to pierce the skin with the hook, or the inner juices will slowly escape while the maggot deflates. Simply nick the point through the 'tab' or appendage that becomes prominent when you squeeze the blunt end. Remember that fine wire hooks puncture far less than thick, forged patterns, which also, being heavier, make the bait fall quicker through the water.

Casters

Under certain circumstances casters are a far more appealing bait than maggots. For the roach or dace in popular, clear-water fisheries that have been well and truly flogged with maggots, the caster will produce more bites and invariably a larger stamp of fish. I believe they are more appealing to cautious fish due to their inherent buoyancy, which, to some degree, offsets the weight of the hook and thus permits a more natural presentation. Indeed, this is proved beyond doubt in certain overfished spots by the fact that regardless of their colour, maggots are totally ignored by the fish, and unless you bait the hook with casters, bites do not happen.

The ideal way to get evenly coloured casters is to

Whether used as sinkers or floaters, casters are a great bait. Try presenting them with a small crust cube to provide extra buoyancy for fishing over weed or a debris-littered bottom.

prepare them from slow-changing maggots in a room at a
low temperature (the garage or garden shed are ideal),
taking them off the ⅛ in wire riddle while they are still
golden yellow. Place them in an open container in the
fridge (other members of the family prefer you to have
your own fridge for this) with a damp towel over them,
which retards colour advancement. Alternatively, immerse
the entire batch in a pail of water for a few minutes
(skimming off any stray floaters), which halts colour
advancement because it kills the animal inside. After
draining off the water, put the casters into a polythene bag
in the fridge. Use them within a few days, before they start
to smell.

I must confess to using old, 'stinky' casters regularly and
not really noticing any depreciation in sport. If you do not
fancy keeping them for hook baits, old casters, whether
they float or not, crunched up into breadcrumbs create a
very attractive groundbait.

All this depends, of course, on preparing a batch of
casters of more or less the same colour, because when
trotting, the loose feed will then all end up in the same part
of the swim. I much prefer to be equipped with a pint or
two of casters of varying colours, or to put it another way,
casters in varying degrees of advancement, because each
will sink at a different rate and I like to offer them all.
Those which have just turned golden yellow, for instance,
will sink quickly to the bottom, while dark brown ones
will float. The latter are best for presentation over dense
bottom weed with just a dust shot to regulate the depth,
and for fishing on the surface for dace and rudd (see
Surface Fishing, p. 104).

Present casters singly on size 18 hooks and smaller by
piercing one end with the point and gently working the
entire hook inside. When fishing two up on a 16 or 14, or
in a bunch covering a size 12 or 10, the hook must go right
through the shell, so be careful.

Caster cocktails, including maggots, sweetcorn, stewed
wheat, elderberries and even bread flake and crust, are well
worth experimenting with. Perhaps the most effective
combination of all, winter or summer, is to trot or present
a slowly falling caster through a swim loose-fed with
hempseed. In cold, clear water conditions it is especially
deadly for shy roach.

Wasp grubs

Of all natural baits, wasp grubs are the most difficult to obtain, and could be dangerous, so be very careful if you decide to take a nest for a supply of the soft, succulent white grubs inside. The grubs are relished by all species, and they should be presented in exactly the same way as maggots, but on larger hooks.

Fruit farmers are plagued by wasps during July and August and spend a considerable amount of time destroying the nests. A polite enquiry in this direction can certainly do no harm. Another source is the local council's pest control unit, or you can always have a go at procuring a nest yourself. Special preparations are available from chemists with explicit instructions that should be followed exactly.

Each nest is about the size of a football and contains several round, honeycomb cakes of about $\frac{1}{4}$ in thick. Those heavy in grubs may be frozen until required, although as they tend to go decidedly 'soft' in the freezer, grubs are always best if used fresh. Three cakes will fit perfectly inside a round, 2 pt maggot tin.

PARTICLE BAITS

Hempseed

One of the most important particles is stewed hempseed, not so much for its hookbait qualities, but because as a loose-feed attractor used in conjunction with numerous hookbait alternatives, its powers are without parallel. To prepare the light grey seeds, put them into a plastic bucket with a rip-off lid and pour over enough boiling water to cover the hemp by at least a couple of inches to allow them to expand. Press the lid on firmly, shake and leave overnight, whereupon any remaining water should be strained off. The noticeably darker seeds, now split with a white shoot protruding, are ready for immediate use.

When preparing hempseed I do a bulk batch of several pints at a time, packing the excess into polybags and into the freezer for future use, a 1 pt bag being quite enough for a day's fishing, even on a large river.

Loose feeding with stewed hempseed should always be done sparingly, especially during the winter months. If you are after river roach or dace, half-a-dozen seeds every other trot down is quite sufficient once the shoal is responding. In swims where hemp is rarely used, or has never been tried, it may take some time for the occupants to respond to this new-found food source, so be patient and be careful not to overfeed.

As I have already mentioned, a single caster presented over loose-fed hemp is a deadly combination, and so, too, is a single maggot, tare, elderberry, or even stewed wheat. Before starting to loose-feed, simply add a handful of the intended hookbait to the bag of hempseed.

The problems arising from using hempseed as a hookbait include that of making it stay on the hook without impairing the strike, and attempting to hit those super-fast bites that invariably result in swims where hemp is used heavily. During the summer months especially, when roach and dace can be seen flashing through clear water as they rise with the speed of light to take the loose seeds (indeed, they can be loose-fed almost to the point of frenzy with hemp) there is the added problem of false bites. When this occurs, cut down drastically on the loose feed, or exchange the lower shots for a length of lead wire twisted around the line 1 ft from the hook and bent over at each end. The seeds may be hooked on by inserting the point of the hook into the base of the seed so that it comes out through the split (the seeds really do have to be well stewed and soft for this), or by pressing the bend of the hook into the split.

Tares

As both loose feed and hook bait, these small, dark, hard seeds do not really have the same pulling power as hemp, but when used in flowing water for dace and roach, they come quite close. To make them soft, preparation is exactly the same as for hemp, except that I prefer to leave them stewing for 48 hours. Tares may also be frozen for later use. One goes nicely on to a size 16 or 14 hook and comes cleanly off on the strike if softened enough in the preparation. As with hemp, loose-feed sparingly and

As a loose feed for roach and dace used in conjunction with either caster, tare, maggot or an elderberry on the hook, stewed hempseed has no equal, summer or winter, in the eyes of many float-fishermen.

experiment with hook-bait alternatives. Tares and elderberry is a winning combination.

Elderberries

Wherever an elder tree hangs out over the water, expect the occupants of the swim beneath to respond to the soft, purple-black elderberries. Used in conjunction with loose-fed hempseed (or tares) elderberries are a wonderful trotting bait for winter roach and dace when the river is that distinct winter green.

If you gather berries in the autumn before they become over-ripe, you can bottle some and use them at any time during the season. Use a screw-top or preserving jar containing a diluted preserving solution of formalin or glycerine, and let small bunches of berries, still on their stalks, drop into it when you cut them with scissors from the main cluster. If you handle the berries individually they might spoil. Take time to rinse the preserving solution out

*Elderberries are a
wonderful trotting bait
for roach and dace.
They can be used at
any time of the season.
During the autumn,
when they are firm,
cut them in to tiny
bunches and preserve
them in a diluted
solution of formalin or
in glycerine.*

of the berries with clean water before you use them as
hook baits, and present one up on a size 16 or 14 hook.

Stewed wheat

During the warmer months especially, when most waters
are loose-fed naturally with grass seed by the wind, not to
mention wildfowlers who attract ducks to the margins by
laying down a grain carpet, stewed wheat is a superb
hookbait in both still and running water.

If you walk miles and miles along a river winding its
way through the most remote farmland to the tiniest of
dykes or feeder streams where anglers never tread, loose-
fed stewed wheat will, in the clearest of water, instantly be
taken by roach, rudd or dace.

There is certainly a special something about the nutty
aroma of stewed wheat, which is prepared quite effectively
in exactly the same way as hempseed except that, because
the grains expand a lot, they must be covered with twice

the volume of boiling water. Once the excess water has been strained from the split grains, revealing the soft white insides, stewed wheat can be used at once or bagged up and frozen for later use. It is such a cheap, effective bait I can never understand why it is not more widely used. Present one grain on a size 14 or three up on a size 10 when you require a real mouthful on the hook to deter immature fish. It is true, however, that stewed wheat on the hook automatically attracts a larger stamp of fish.

Sweetcorn

Just like wheat, sweetcorn is definitely a bait of the summer and a great alternative to bread in all its forms for seeking larger specimens. Stillwater rudd and roach quickly respond to sweetcorn, as indeed do river fish.

On the last occasion that I fished the famous Royalty Fishery in Christchurch on the Hampshire Avon for its legendary barbel, there was a period when I almost wished I had opted to catch dace. So many fine specimens up to 10 oz plus were coming to ledgered sweetcorn, I was indeed tempted to change over completely to ultra-light float tackle and forget the barbel.

If you intend using a fair amount of sweetcorn, it is cheaper to purchase it in large freezer packs rather than by the tin. Another benefit is that individual kernels in freezer packs are larger and not so soft. Sweetcorn lends itself wonderfully to the presentation of cocktail baits, so experiment by adding a caster or two, a tiny redworm, a couple of maggots, or even a small piece of bread crust. When fish are finicky in clear water or during the heat and brightness of a summer day, these little differences can create an instant response.

Peanuts

I have given peanuts a special category here because I have caught a lot of prime roach and rudd by using them. As I mentioned at the beginning of the chapter, virtually any food, so long as enough is introduced, is liable to be taken seriously by these three species. In the well-known carp fishery at Homersfield on the Norfolk/Suffolk border owned by my good friend, Norman Symonds, huge roach up to and even over the magical 3 lb mark are regularly taken on heavy tackle baited with large 14 to 18 mm boilies intended for carp. However, I am certainly not suggesting that a ledgered large boilie is the method for catching big roach.

To prepare peanuts follow the instructions for stewed hempseed and allow them to stew for two days before use.

BREAD

When thinking in terms of catching larger-than-average roach and rudd, including the real monsters, or if you wish simply to evade tiddlers that continually gorge themselves on maggots, then both winter and summer look no further than a thumbnail-sized piece of soft white bread flake from the inside of a really fresh loaf hiding a size 8 or even a 6 hook. Such a large mouthful automatically takes your bait through the unwanted smaller fish down to the specimens, wherever you fish.

My preference is for ready-sliced loaves packed in polythene bags, which seem to stay fresh longer. However, to be fully confident when using bread flake, and that after a short while you are not simply sitting there with a bare hook because the flake has disintegrated, use only fresh white doughy bread. You can certainly help bread flake stay on longer by compressing it really hard around only the hook shank, between thumb and forefinger, while masking the point and barb with the thumb of your other hand. This ensures that the flake remains fluffy and swells to an attractive carnation shape, hiding what lies beneath. Penetration on the strike is then never impaired.

Flake also works well when used in a cocktail. To the bend of the hook try adding a grain of wheat, two maggots or casters; to increase buoyancy for fishing into or over heavy weed, add a piece of bread crust.

Breadcrust

As with flake, use the crust from a new loaf. While it will not stay on anywhere near as long as flake or paste, because

There is no finer or cheaper hook bait for use during the summer months than stewed wheat. Not only does it sort out the quality fish, it is easy to prepare, clean to use and may be ledgered, layed on or trotted.

The pulling power of sweetcorn is not confined to tench and carp. Dace, roach and rudd readily accept it, during the summer months especially, whether presented on its own or as a maggot and corn cocktail. The latter accounted for this fine rudd.

of its greater buoyancy, there are numerous occasions when crust scores over all else.

You have the option of removing all four sides from a tin loaf with a bread knife and dicing each into cubes, or removing the crusts of a cut loaf slice by slice from the wrapper when required. The latter method helps keep the remainder of the loaf fresh in warm weather. As for actual cube size, remember that crust swells to at least half as large again once wet, so choose the hook size accordingly. A balanced bait of an oblong of crust along the shank and

If I were limited to just one bait for luring only specimen roach or rudd, it would be plain, fresh, white bread, either flake or a cube of crust, ledgered or long-trotted beneath a chunky float.

The open-ended swimfeeder packed with caster- or maggot-laced breadcrumbs that have been only lightly dampened, explodes its load in an attractive cloud around the hook bait when the rig hits bottom. Over-wet the crumbs, and they will clog in the feeder.

maggots or casters or even flake on the bend, for instance, permits a wonderfully natural on-the-drop presentation. Crust obviously scores when you are fishing over a really uneven, snaggy or weedy bottom.

Bread paste

To ring the changes from flake and crust when after quality-sized roach and rudd, try a lump of creamy white bread paste, which is easy to make from all your old stale bread scraps. In fact, it is impossible to make a good paste from new, doughy bread.

Start by removing all the crusts (the bread needs to be at least four or five days old) and hold the bread under the cold water tap for several seconds. Next, knead it (with clean hands) until all the stickiness disappears and the paste becomes pliable without lumps. Wrapped in a damp cloth, bread paste will stay fresh for at least 24 hours, and can be frozen for future use.

Punched bread

Fresh, white, sliced bread is the best to use when punching out pellets. Don't forget to take along a rigid board to press the bread against.

GROUNDBAITS

Mashed bread

Whether using punched bread while floatfishing, or a large piece of ledgered bread flake, by far the best groundbait is mashed bread. For this, use stale bread of at least 5 or 6 days old and soak it for a couple of hours in a bucket of water. After straining off the excess water, squeeze and mash the bread (hence its name) between your fingers into a fine pulp.

Prior to throwing it into the swim, squeeze the mash again and mould it into the size of balls required.

Naturally, the tighter you squeeze and mould the mash, the further it sinks before breaking up into a cascade of attractive feed. If you merely desire a cloud to complement the use of tiny, punched bread pellets when canal fishing for small roach or rudd, keep the mash on the sloppy side and introduce it in tiny balls. At the other end of the scale, to stiffen the mash groundbait so it quickly descends to the bottom of deep, fast swims, add maize meal, bran or even dry breadcrumbs, plus a few fragments of the bait if you are not using bread on the hook.

Breadcrumbs

Breadcrumbs form the base of many commercially-made groundbaits, which, for the smaller species such as roach, rudd and dace, also contain attractors like ground hempseed. Crumbs make the best groundbait for fishing with a cage or open-ended, plastic swimfeeder, whether it is completely filled or used with a crumb plug at each end and a hookbait fragment filling of maggots, casters, wheat, and so on.

The secret lies in not over-wetting the crumbs or they will clog and refuse to release until the feeder is retrieved. If merely dampened, the crumbs explode and scatter attractively around the hookbait as the feeder touches bottom. Practise in the margins until you get the balance right.

For throwing by hand, add water a little at a time to the crumbs, fluffing them around in the bottom of a bait bowl or tray until they just hold together with a light squeeze. Then add a handful of hookbait fragments. Aim for a consistency which, with a really firm squeeze, holds together and sinks well, breaking up only when it reaches the bottom. With a little practice you can make breadcrumb groundbait behave just as you want. It is all down to the way it is mixed and squeezed.

During the winter months, when the water is clear and low temperatures reduce the metabolism of roach, rudd and dace to a level where they consume far less natural food and so are more interested in much smaller baits, there is little point in providing them with any more than loose-fed fragments of the hookbait.

CHAPTER SEVEN

TECHNIQUES AND RIGS

FREELINING

Streams and small rivers

The art of freelining the bait in smaller rivers and clear flowing streams to catch quality roach and the odd sizeable dace is based upon concealment, and is most effective during the summer months when fish are really active. You need to creep and crawl stealthily about in order to get close to the quarry, so that you can flick the bait out a few yards – or even feet.

On open waters you can get away with using a 12 ft carbon float rod, but wherever the banks are heavily overgrown, and the most interesting and prolific diminutive rivers usually are, a long rod is an encumberance. My choice is a 10–11 ft built-in quivertip ledger rod. While you are not always watching the rod tip for indications, simply the line (as the word 'freelining' implies), the bait does at times need to be anchored on the bottom with a swanshot or two. And this is when the sensitive quivertip comes into its own.

All the weight for casting (pinching on a shot 12 in above light baits such as maggots is permitted) is of course in the bait itself, which will easily peel line from the spool providing it is full to the brim with around 2½ lb test. Do not forget to adjust the slipping clutch, because freelined large baits – and there is nothing better than a large lump of bread flake hiding a size 10 or 8 hook tied direct – really does sort out the better quality roach.

Groundbait is of course quite unnecessary. To get the fish interested, flick in a few hookbait samples every so often. Search all the likely-looking spots where you would expect roach to be in residence (see Chapter Four), paying particular attention to raft swims where flotsam and cut

weed collect around trailing willow or alder branches, creating a large canopy over the surface.

After pinching the flake on, 'dunk' it momentarily at your feet to make sure it sinks (dunking also makes it heavier), then flick it downstream, a few feet up from the raft, and allow the current to drift it beneath the raft. Keep a bow in the line from the rod tip to the point where the line enters the water and watch it like a hawk. It is your resistance-free bite indicator.

Even bites from 10 oz roach will look like a shark run. As the fish senses no fear from the food it is swallowing, due to a complete lack of terminal gear, it will grab it confidently, the line straightening in a ridiculously positive manner. If the roach decides to turn around and swim to a position at the rear of the shoal, the rod tip will even pull round. And if it chews the flake on the spot the line may only jerk forward momentarily once or twice.

There is of course nothing to stop you adding a shot to anchor the bait, which is how specimen roach often want it. Bites of course are registered in exactly the same way. Freelining is a roving, searching technique where you can never sit back and relax. Take only essential items of tackle along, plus a selection of hooks and shots stored in your waistcoat pocket or you will be loathe to explore each and every swim.

Snuggled low down among dense marginal rushes, David Wilson practises the art of freelining by watching the bow in his line like a hawk, while the bait – a large piece of bread flake on a size 8 hook – trundles through a clear run along the opposite bank.

Stillwater freelining

In stillwaters, freelining is practised in exactly the same way to catch quality roach and rudd on large baits from close-range swims, among lilies and such like, simply by watching the bow in the line. Rod-rests, electronic alarms or other indicators are not required. Rudd will sometimes intercept buoyant baits like bread flake so fast while it is sinking slowly that the rod tip bangs before you have reacted to the bow tightening. It is great fun at dusk when the biggest rudd of all put in an appearance, and you can easily detect bites once the light has gone completely by holding a loop of line gently between butt ring and reel in your non-rod hand. When the bait is grabbed you will feel a certain heaviness and strike automatically.

LEDGERING

Quivertipping in running water

There are two important points to remember when planning to catch roach and dace (and rudd if you fish in southern Ireland) on the quivertip in running water. Choose the most sensitive quivertip to match current strength in order that even tentative bites will register (see Tackle, p. 61). Secondly, use the minimum weight, whether swan shots, bomb or feeder, so that drop-back bites are always indicated. Smaller species do not have the strength to move a heavy bomb or feeder and indicate a drop-back bite on the quivertip should they move across the flow and upstream with the bait. So make sure you anchor the bait with only just enough weight and no more.

You must also decide whether to introduce loose feed or groundbait or both, by feeder, or by hand. When fishing clear flowing small rivers during the summer months, for instance, where swims and even the position of the shoal is clearly defined, the answer is to flick in a few fragments of hookbait every so often by hand or catapult – pieces of flake, stewed wheat, maggots and so on. Indeed, throw in too much free food and your sport might end prematurely, as it is easy to overfeed the fish unintentionally.

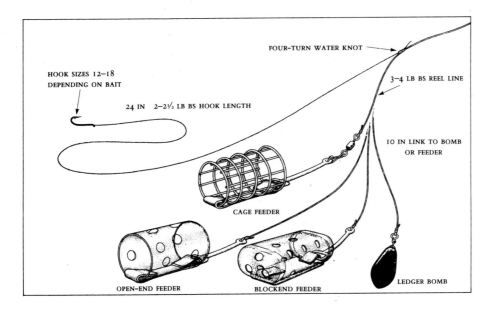

FOUR-TURN WATER KNOT

HOOK SIZES 12–18
DEPENDING ON BAIT

3–4 LB BS REEL LINE

24 IN   2–2½ LB BS HOOK LENGTH

10 IN LINK TO BOMB
OR FEEDER

CAGE FEEDER

OPEN-END FEEDER   BLOCKEND FEEDER   LEDGER BOMB

FIGURE 8 *Basic quivertip ledger rig for river fishing*

Through clear water it is sometimes possible to see how many fish there are in the swim and to observe how roach and dace react to free food. You can then regulate the feed exactly to match their mood and appetite. There is a problem of course, when ledgering in coloured water or into distant, clear-water swims, where the size of the shoal cannot be seen – which, let us face it, is most of the time. My advice is to underfeed rather than overfeed the fish.

In large rivers where shoals might number several hundreds rather than dozens, and competition for food is high, loose feed or groundbait deposited by swimfeeder with the hookbait each cast is imperative for constant sport. See fig. 8 for the various rig options.

Incidentally, when ledgering into deep water or for casting a feeder out 30 to 40 yd plus, I prefer the safety margin provided by a 4 lb reel-line. Otherwise a 3 lb reel-line is quite sufficient. To keep a massive shoal of roach feeding in the fast, deep waters of Norfolk's tidal rivers Bure, Yare and Waveney, or the River Bann in Northern Ireland, you have the option of using a cage or open-end feeder packed with maggot- or caster-laced breadcrumbs, or a blockend feeder holding maggots or casters only. On some days roach will respond better to the addition of cereals, some days they will not. If in doubt, stick to a blockend and loose feed only.

The rewards of
quivertipping in cold,
flowing water. John
used a Drennan
feeder-link, blockend
to distribute loose feed
and to hold the double
maggot bait static on
the bottom of a local
mill-pool to capture
this splendid winter
roach.

For attracting the roach living on the bottom of a fast
and deep weir-pool into a given area, the blockend
certainly reigns supreme. The cereal/open-end or cage
feeder combination is more likely to scatter fish all over the
swim because the crumb particles are so light that they
disperse a long way. And in winter conditions, when you
need to really concentrate the shoal into a small area, this
could prove disastrous. And unless your casting is consistently accurate, the same thing will happen.

For dace that inhabit really fast swims, the blockend and
maggot or caster combination is certainly more productive
(use a small blockend for dace). It is worth remembering
that in strong currents the blockend's load (even casters)
will wash out much quicker than in slow currents. For fast
water, therefore, choose a blockend with a limited amount
of small holes for slow dispersal of the bait. In slow swims,
go for the reverse – a feeder well punched with large holes.

As a keeper on Berkshire's famous River Kennet, David Culley knows all about big dace. Like many others taken during the winter months when the river is up and heavily coloured, this one accepted maggots ledgered in conjunction with a blockend feeder.

Some feeder manufacturers offer weights of alternative sizes for their feeders. The Drennan Feederlink (a great blockend for slow-moving water), for example, has a plastic spigot at the bottom to which different weights of between 1/8 and 1/2 oz can be clipped. It is handy to have a supply of fold-over or strap leads in varying sizes from 1/2 to 2 oz so that any make of cage, open-end or blockend feeder, can be doctored to hold bottom regardless of current strength (within reason). As I mentioned previously, the object is for the feeder (or ledger weight) to only just hold bottom, so it can easily be dislodged by a biting fish to register a drop-back on the quivertip.

As many anglers are unsure about which position the rod should be placed in when quivertipping in flowing water, I think a few words are in order. As can be seen from fig. 9A, in small rivers where the line more or less follows the flow downstream between tip and bait, point

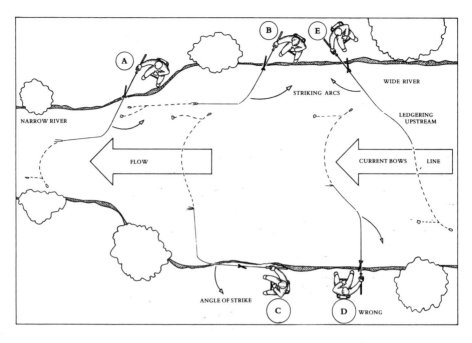

FIGURE 9 *Correct*
positioning of the rod
when quivertipping in
flowing water

the rod outwards and angled slightly downstream, so that
an upstream strike pulls the line through the correct ark.
Adopt the same position for large rivers when fishing at
close range into the bank, as in fig. 9B. When fishing way
out across the flow, however, you must sit facing
downstream with the rod almost parallel to the river, as in
fig. 9C, so that the strike pulls the line through a similar
ark to the sub-surface bow created by the current. Fig. 9D
shows how, with the rod positioned straight out (wrong),
insufficient line is moved on the strike.

When upstream ledgering, sit facing the river with the
rod angled slightly upstream, as in fig. 9E. Note that the
striking ark closely follows the way the line lies beneath
the surface. Bites must be struck through this ark for the
maximum amount of line to be straightened. If not, many
bites will be missed.

The advantage of quivertipping upstream is that it
allows you to reach choice areas along your own bank, or
along the opposite bank where fish cannot be reached by
casting downstream because overhanging trees, snags or
reed-beds restrict your access. Such swims are ignored by
most anglers, so the occupants are invariably more
receptive and bite with more confidence than those in all
the more popular, and consequently overfished, swims.

If you use just enough weight to hold bottom when a fish grabs the bait, the weight is instantly dislodged and the quivertip springs back suddenly, at which point you should make a sweeping, powerful strike in order to pick up the slack line. Keep the rod-tip up high at all times or current pressure on that extra line beneath the surface (if you lower the tip) will dislodge the ledger and cause false bites.

When presenting bread flake for quality river roach, use a plastic, open-ended or cage feeder packed with breadcrumbs – unless fishing at close range, when the breadcrumbs or mashed-bread groundbait (see Ground-baits, p. 84) can in all but the strongest currents be introduced by hand. If the latter is the case, a simple swan shot or bomb ledger will suffice and create less disturbance, especially to crafty old roach (see fig. 10). Whenever I present ledgered bread flake to the specimen roach in my local reaches of the Upper Wensum, for instance, where the shoals are small, containing perhaps no more than a dozen or two members, I introduce a few balls of mashed bread only at the start, to get them interested, not with every cast.

Bites on ledgered bread flake from roach of about 1 lb upwards are, in all except the lowest temperatures, positive indications on the quivertip – slow pull-rounds following an initial tap or two, or a drop-back that could be anything between a sudden straightening of the tip, to the merest suggestion of the ledger resettling – the tip

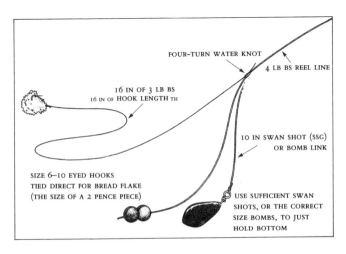

FIGURE 10 *Simple fixed paternoster for big roach or rudd in rivers*

FOUR-TURN WATER KNOT

4 LB BS REEL LINE

16 IN OF 3 LB BS
16 IN OF HOOK LENGTH TH

10 IN SWAN SHOT (SSG)
OR BOMB LINK

SIZE 6–10 EYED HOOKS
TIED DIRECT FOR BREAD FLAKE
(THE SIZE OF A 2 PENCE PIECE)

USE SUFFICIENT SWAN
SHOTS, OR THE CORRECT
SIZE BOMBS, TO JUST
HOLD BOTTOM

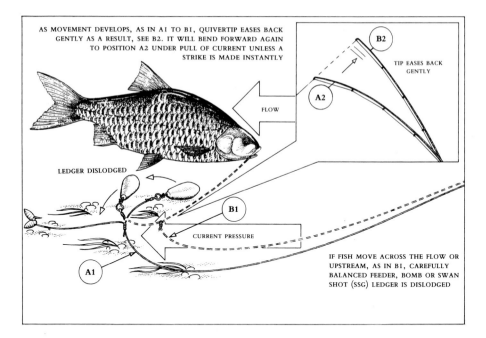

AS MOVEMENT DEVELOPS, AS IN A1 TO B1, QUIVERTIP EASES BACK GENTLY AS A RESULT, SEE B2. IT WILL BEND FORWARD AGAIN TO POSITION A2 UNDER PULL OF CURRENT UNLESS A STRIKE IS MADE INSTANTLY

B2

TIP EASES BACK GENTLY

A2

FLOW

LEDGER DISLODGED

B1

A1

CURRENT PRESSURE

IF FISH MOVE ACROSS THE FLOW OR UPSTREAM, AS IN B1, CAREFULLY BALANCED FEEDER, BOMB OR SWAN SHOT (SSG) LEDGER IS DISLODGED

FIGURE 11
Identifying gentle drop-back bites on the quivertip in rivers

gently easing back a ¼ in and no more before moving forward again to the pull of the current. This is why it is so important to use only just enough weight to hold bottom. It allows you to identify and strike to many bites that on a heavier, less sensitive ledger rig would not even be seen (see fig. 11).

Current pressure on the line really is the all-important factor, and is the main difference between quivertip ledgering in flowing and stillwater. In the strong currents of weir-pools, or when ledgering way out across a wide river, unless you keep the tip well up supported on a front rest to keep most of the line above the surface, the tip will pull round to current force alone. Even worse, the bait will be pulled slowly away from the line of feed to which the shoal has been attracted. Conversely, when quivertipping in extremely slow currents, if the quivertip is positioned within inches of the surface tentative bites will be very much easier to see. Indeed, in windy weather this is the only way of seeing them.

The target board designed for match fishing is an extremely useful aid to seeing tiny tip movements when roach or dace are biting tentatively, as is the case in very low water temperatures. You can make your own easily enough, or purchase a ready-made board, but be sure it is

John's striking hand hovers over the rod handle, daring the quivertip to bend round a little further. In cold conditions (note the vacuum flask standing on marginal ice) bites from roach and dace could show as mere trembles on the quivertip. Note also how the butt ring is locked over the front rod-rest, which keeps the rod very steady and returns it to the same position after every cast.

reversible with angled lines on both sides to accommodate fishing to either the right or the left. The target board should be positioned a few inches behind the tip so that after tightening up to the ledger, the slightest tremble shows against the marker lines because *both* are in sharp focus. This is impossible if the board is placed too far away.

Springtipping

The springtip can be used most effectively in conjunction with the target board (see Tackle, p. 61). This indicator is great in really gentle currents for shy-biting fish, especially dace, when you need to step down to really fine hook lengths and tiny hooks. Use the board in the same way as the quivertip.

Quivertipping for specimens at night

Both summer and winter, the very best opportunity for
latching on to a really big river roach, especially in clear
water conditions, is by quivertipping during the hours of
darkness. Wily old roach that only an hour beforehand
would not look at a single maggot unless presented on a
gossamer line and 24 hook, will gobble up a large piece of
bread flake once darkness sets in. And if you want a big
roach, use a size 8 hook tied direct to a 3 lb hook link.
During the winter months, I prefer to wait for mild
conditions that coincide with a rip-roaring flood, with a
view to fishing on a couple of consecutive evenings once
water levels have returned almost to normal and while the
river still holds that sandy-green colour with a visibility of
no more than 1 ft or so. If you lose sight of a maggot or
piece of bread flake when it has only sunk 1 ft beneath the
surface, you can be fishing at no better time.

Fish will still bite once the water clears, of course, and
even during freezing conditions, but nowhere near so
aggressively as immediately after a flood. It is almost as
though they have not fed during the full force of the flood
while the water is heavy with debris, rotten weed and
residues entering the river from drainage dykes and so on.
However, they become ravenous as the flood subsides.

To help matters along, and if I can find the time, I pre-
bait for a couple of evenings prior to fishing with several
balls of mashed bread, squeezed really tightly so they go
straight down and settle on the bottom of the swim.

It makes sense when fishing after dark to arrive while
there is still enough light to set up and familiarize yourself
with the swim and flow patterns, and to introduce some
mashed bread. Set up the rod with the quivertip high,
pointing out and slightly downstream on a pair of rests so
the butt ring hooks over the front rest and thus returns to
exactly the same spot after each cast. Then cast out and
allow the tip to take on its gentle curve with the current
once the ledger has settled. A simple swan shot paternoster
rig is perfect (see fig. 10).

Position a narrow-beam torch a few feet downstream so
that it shines outwards and upstream, illuminating only the
white quivertip and not the surface of the water. With the
tip illuminated in this way, you can watch in a relaxed yet

expectant manner for several hours without eye strain and without ruining your night vision, and strike at even diminutive bites – although, as I have already said, bites from sizeable roach after dark are invariably extremely bold, as are large river rudd. Big dace also respond well after dark and just when the light is going. I use bread flake until the early autumn and the first frosts, and then reduce the bait size to maggots and casters on smaller hooks.

Quivertipping in stillwaters

Bites from roach and rudd in stillwaters on the quivertip are rarely as bold as those in running water, because river fish are used to resistance while those in stillwaters are not. Nevertheless, when trying to combat a strong sub-surface tow, or fishing into really deep water, the quivertip is the ideal indicator. Select the most sensitive tip (see Tackle, p. 61) that conditions will permit. And to alleviate wind resistance, position the rod on two rod-rests angled either to the right or left (whichever is more comfortable) so that you can follow through along the identical line with a long sweeping strike. The tip should be no more than 12 in above the water surface. If the water is shallow strike really low to the surface, and if deep strike upwards. Each will pull the maximum amount of line through the surface film to set the hook.

As when river fishing for large shoals of fish, a swimfeeder rig greatly increases your chances of drawing them into a small area and encouraging them to bite regularly. During the summer and autumn, use an open-end or cage feeder with a filling of crumb plus hookbait samples – stewed wheat, corn, casters, maggots and so on. Try bread flake or crust if specimens are expected or known to exist. For winter fishing in freezing conditions, when sport is quite liable to be extremely slow in still water, restrict the amount of loose feed by swapping the open-end feeder for a blockend, which permits a very slow dispersal of baits like casters and maggots. If bites are not forthcoming, or sucked maggots are occasionally experienced without a noticeable indication on the tip, reduce the hook-link length to just 6–10 in and hooks down to sizes 18–20 (see fig. 12).

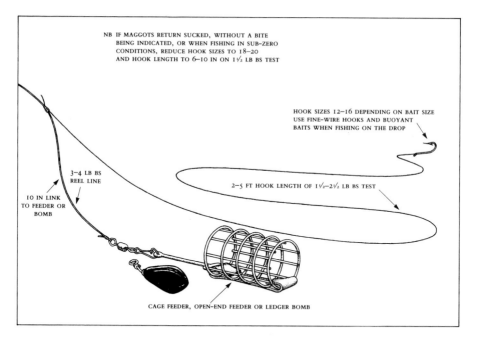

NB IF MAGGOTS RETURN SUCKED, WITHOUT A BITE
BEING INDICATED, OR WHEN FISHING IN SUB-ZERO
CONDITIONS, REDUCE HOOK SIZES TO 18–20
AND HOOK LENGTH TO 6–10 IN ON 1½ LB BS TEST

HOOK SIZES 12–16 DEPENDING ON BAIT SIZE
USE FINE-WIRE HOOKS AND BUOYANT
BAITS WHEN FISHING ON THE DROP

3–4 LB BS
REEL LINE

10 IN LINK
TO FEEDER OR
BOMB

2–5 FT HOOK LENGTH OF 1½–2½ LB BS TEST

CAGE FEEDER, OPEN-END FEEDER OR LEDGER BOMB

FIGURE 12 *Stillwater quivertip or swingtip ledger rig*

If the bait is inched slowly along the bottom every so often by giving the reel handle half a turn, this will sometimes spur lethargic fish into grabbing the bait. Buoyant baits work especially well with this technique. Try a couple of maggots on the bend with an oblong crust on the shank of the hook, or a maggot and dark (buoyant) caster duo. If bottom debris such as rotten weed proves troublesome use two or three buoyant casters only (see Casters, p. 74).

Using the swingtip in still and slow-moving water

In terms of rigs and baits, everything is exactly the same with swingtipping as with quivertipping. Remember, however, that swingtips are effective only in still and very slow-moving water. To counteract even the slightest current, or a stillwater sub-surface tow, you must use a loaded swingtip (see Tackle, p. 60). For most situations, a lightweight 10–12 in swingtip is fine and will, due to the angle at which the tip dangles or hangs once you have tightened up to the terminal rig, register the tiniest of bites

Small wonder Martin Founds is smiling. Big roach are not avid biters in bright conditions, but by using a feeder rig, so his bait lay among the loose feed, and scaling down to an 18 hook holding a single bronze maggot, the super-sensitive quivertip registered hittable bites.

with the bare minimum of resistance. So the swingtip is especially suited to small and shy-biting fish.

You can sit facing the water with the rod pointing straight out at an angle, as when quivertipping, or sit with the rod parallel to the water. Most swingtippers prefer to sit with the rod parallel because a target board can then be fixed into the bank immediately in front of the tip (see p. 61), which allows the tiniest tip movements to be seen. This, of course, is impossible with the rod pointing straight out over the water.

The swingtip is by far the best indicator for registering drop-back bites where the fish inhales the bait as it is sinking. Small baits on tiny hooks complement this method because they descend much slower to the bottom. To really slow down a single maggot for example, add a dark (buoyant) caster or present a cube of bread crust. Experimentation will create numerous chances.

Put the rod in the rests quickly after casting (I prefer to use just a front rest and to lay the butt across my knee for a quick response), and immediately tighten up to the bomb or feeder once it hits bottom. Watch the tip intently. While it slowly drops backwards after each turn of the reel handle and until the tip finally hangs, any noticeable delay means the bait has been taken on the drop. Strike at once in a smooth follow-through style.

To encourage a really slow fall, use a light hook length – about 1½ lb test – somewhere between 2 and 5 ft long, and a small fine-wire hook (see fig. 12). If nothing takes the bait on the drop, the tip will rise once it is sucked up from the bottom, unless the fish moves towards the rod and dislodges the bomb or feeder, in which case the swingtip will fall back. Strike instantly at either indication.

Long-range ledgering in stillwaters

When ledgering in search of roach and rudd in large stillwaters, which often means placing the bait at distances of 50 yd and further into deep water, I use bobbin bite indicators. These clip on to the line between the reel and the butt ring (see Tackle, p. 62). If I expect sport to be slow, I use a two-rod set-up and incorporate electronic bite indicators as the front rod-rests.

Rods are 11 or 12 ft standard tip, carbon Avons coupled to a 4 lb reel-line. This may seem a little heavy, but continually casting a heavy bomb or feeder rig can drastically weaken lighter tests. In addition, the stretch in 50 yd of lighter line would inhibit hook penetration, especially large hooks of size 10 and above so necessary for presenting bread flake. The standard fixed paternoster (with feeder or bomb) is employed with a lighter hook length of around 2 lb test and hooks in sizes 16 to 12 if using baits like maggots with a feeder rig.

Increase the hook link to 3 lb for larger hooks and baits. Sizes 10 and 8 with bread flake or crust are perfect and attract a much larger stamp of fish when tiddlers prove troublesome. When using bread on the hook, use crumb only in an open-end feeder.

Night fishing with large bread baits is the best way of coming to grips with specimen rudd and roach. Do not be scared of using a 2p-sized piece of bread flake covering a size 6 hook. It really does sort out the big fish.

Retain the two-rod set-up and for bite indication use the luminous 'glo bobbins', which should be hung between butt ring and reel on a drop of around 18 in. If there is any appreciable underwater tow or surface chop, steady the bobbins by pinching a swan shot or two on the retaining cord immediately below each bobbin. Lastly, eradicate all possible resistance to a biting fish (other than the bobbin) by pointing the rod directly at the bait with the tip angled downwards. Pre-bait an hour before dark with mashed bread when summer fishing, if distance permits. If not, rely on the two crumb-filled feeders for attraction. Just an hour's fishing with two rods regularly putting the feeders out to the same area can lay down a fair carpet of loose feed.

FLOAT FISHING

For modest-sized species like roach, rudd and dace, where possible I would always choose to present the bait beneath a float rather than by ledgering, because the tiniest bites can be struck and the bait can be offered in a most natural manner anywhere between the surface and bottom.

STILLWATER FLOAT FISHING

Light rigs

To catch roach and rudd from small stillwaters, or when the shoal is fairly close into the margins of large lakes and pits, there is nothing to beat the joy of light float fishing using a 13 ft waggler-style rod and a 2 lb reel line.

I suggest a simple multi-purpose rig as shown in fig. 13A incorporating a fine-tipped antenna (such as a stillwater green or blue) holding two No. 1 for calm water or taking up to 3AA for windy conditions. The stability provided by

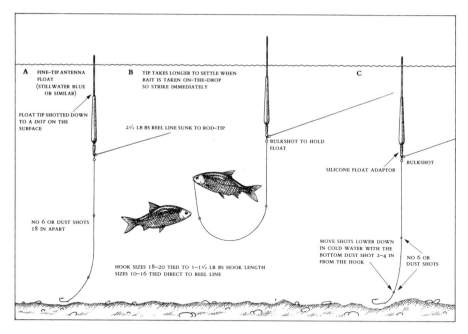

A FINE-TIP ANTENNA
FLOAT
(STILLWATER BLUE
OR SIMILAR)

FLOAT TIP SHOTTED DOWN
TO A *DOT* ON THE
SURFACE

B TIP TAKES LONGER TO SETTLE WHEN
BAIT IS TAKEN ON-THE-DROP
SO STRIKE IMMEDIATELY

C

2½ LB BS REEL LINE SUNK TO ROD-TIP

BULKSHOT TO HOLD
FLOAT

SILICONE FLOAT ADAPTOR   BULKSHOT

NO 6 OR DUST SHOTS
18 IN APART

HOOK SIZES 18–20 TIED TO 1–1½ LB BS HOOK LENGTH
SIZES 10–16 TIED DIRECT TO REEL LINE

MOVE SHOTS LOWER DOWN
IN COLD WATER WITH THE
BOTTOM DUST SHOT 2–4 IN
FROM THE HOOK

NO 6 OR
DUST SHOTS

FIGURE 13 *Light,
multi-purpose
stillwater rig*

*Presenting casters just
beyond the marginal
shelf using a sensitive
'stillwater green' rig
shotted down so that
the merest tip showed,
Dave Thomas was
soon among a shoal of
quality winter roach
in this popular
stillwater.*

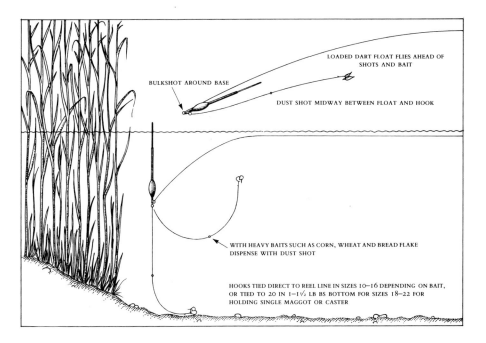

LOADED DART FLOAT FLIES AHEAD OF
SHOTS AND BAIT

BULKSHOT AROUND BASE

DUST SHOT MIDWAY BETWEEN FLOAT AND HOOK

WITH HEAVY BAITS SUCH AS CORN, WHEAT AND BREAD FLAKE
DISPENSE WITH DUST SHOT

HOOKS TIED DIRECT TO REEL LINE IN SIZES 10–16 DEPENDING ON BAIT,
OR TIED TO 20 IN 1–1½ LB BS BOTTOM FOR SIZES 18–22 FOR
HOLDING SINGLE MAGGOT OR CASTER

FIGURE 14 Dart rig for fishing on the drop

the body allows you to shot the sensitive tip down to the merest dot so that the tiniest bite registers.

Plumb the swim carefully so the bait just comes to rest on the bottom once the two shots have settled. A bite can be determined at any time throughout the bait's descent (as in fig. 13B), or once it comes to rest on the bottom. Should the majority of bites happen on the drop because the shoal is situated in the upper water layers (most typical of summer rudd), move the float down and try various levels. In really deep water, say 10–12 ft or deeper, the layer at which the shoal holds may change at any time, so when bites slow up try different levels until you relocate the main shoal. Remember to cast well beyond the area you are loose feeding, and dip the rod tip beneath the surface while cranking the reel handle a few turns in order to sink the line. This is a most important procedure for all stillwater float fishing, otherwise any slight draw or chop on the surface will drag the rig, and thus the bait, along unnaturally.

In really cold water conditions, move both dust shots lower down with the bottom one just 2–4 in from the hook, and strike at the very slightest indication, no matter how insignificant (see fig. 13C). When deliberately presenting the bait on the drop to rudd or roach patrolling tight up against marginal reeds along the opposite bank of a canal or a reed promontory reaching out into the lake, use a small, loaded float such as a zoomer or a dart, which sails through the air ahead of the bait (see fig. 14). The secret when fishing on the drop is to catapult the loose feed out and cast over it immediately, so that both bait and feed sink simultaneously.

With heavy baits, use no shot on the line. A single caster or maggot may need the addition of a dust shot midway between float and hook. The bait is quite liable to be sucked in at any second from the moment it hits the surface, so be ready.

Surface fishing

When roach and rudd are working the upper water layers during the summer months, and are more interested in sucking in food from the surface, make up a flat peacock quill rig, as in fig. 15. Fix the entire shotting load at each end of the float and strike when it glides across the surface as opposed to going under. This is a rig that creates the minimum resistance to surface takers.

FIGURE 15 *The flat peacock quill rig for surface fishing*

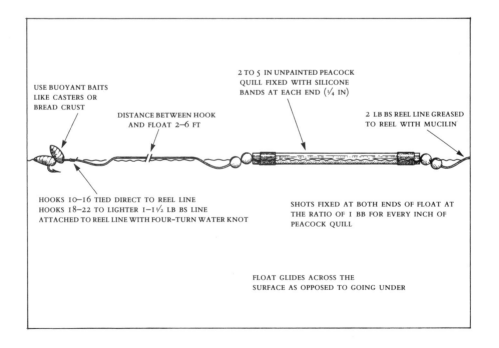

USE BUOYANT BAITS
LIKE CASTERS OR
BREAD CRUST

DISTANCE BETWEEN HOOK
AND FLOAT 2–6 FT

2 TO 5 IN UNPAINTED PEACOCK
QUILL FIXED WITH SILICONE
BANDS AT EACH END (¼ IN)

2 LB BS REEL LINE GREASED
TO REEL WITH MUCILIN

HOOKS 10–16 TIED DIRECT TO REEL LINE
HOOKS 18–22 TO LIGHTER 1–1½ LB BS LINE
ATTACHED TO REEL LINE WITH FOUR-TURN WATER KNOT

SHOTS FIXED AT BOTH ENDS OF FLOAT AT
THE RATIO OF 1 BB FOR EVERY INCH OF
PEACOCK QUILL

FLOAT GLIDES ACROSS THE
SURFACE AS OPPOSED TO GOING UNDER

At close quarters it is often possible to watch the bait being sucked in and to forget the float altogether. Just remember not to allow too much of a bow to develop between rod and float, otherwise striking could be impaired. A good dubbing of mucilin on the line will ensure that it floats well, allowing you to lift and mend the line every so often.

To loose feed, catapult fragments a little in front of the rig and slowly draw your hookbait among them. Casters are the perfect bait for this technique, but make sure they are all floaters or you might discourage the rudd from surface feeding. Loose-fed scraps of bread crust catapulted well upwind also attract rudd, and when they start splashing and nibbling at the bread use a small cube of bread crust on the hook. A deadly method of luring the real specimens is to present a large lump of bread flake on the hook, which sinks below all the surface activity to the larger, more cautious rudd down below. Give it a try. If the flake is sucked in when it has sunk several feet below the surface (raise the float to allow for depth), the flat float will zoom under in the normal manner.

Waggler fishing at medium- to long-range in stillwater

For presenting the bait to roach and rudd way out in large stillwaters, where casting distance or choppy conditions immediately rule out the light rigs already mentioned, the float to use is the tipped waggler. It can be shotted to offer the bait on the drop or at any depth from a few feet beneath the surface to hard on the bottom (as in fig. 16 A and B).

A good general rig is shown in fig. 16A, with the bulk shot required to reach the swim grouped around the float so that it casts like an arrow, leaving two small shots down the line near the hook. If you plumb the swim carefully so the bait just touches bottom at the end of its fall, bites on the drop will register by the float tip failing to settle in its final position, and at any time afterwards when the bait touches bottom. In really cold water, when rudd and roach occupy the lower water layers, the bait might need to be nailed to the lake-bed to indicate a bite. If so, then fish

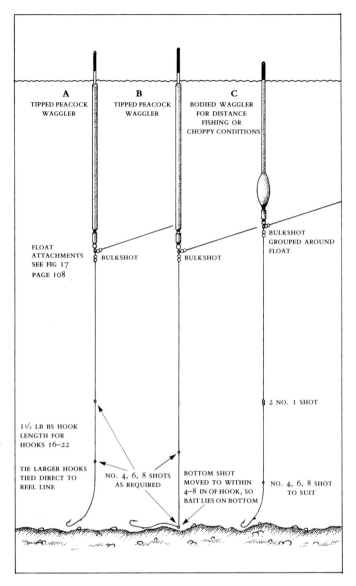

FIGURE 16 *Stillwater*
peacock waggler rigs

slightly over depth and juggle about with the lower shots,
ensuring the bottom one is somewhere between 4 to 8 in
from the hook (as in fig. 16B).

At all times remember to overcast and wind the float
back over the shoal with the rod tip below the surface to
ensure that the line is sunk.

For the often long and continual casting involved in
waggler fishing in stillwater, I increase the reel-line
strength to 2½ lb test and use a 14 ft rod for long-distance

A waggler or dart rig with the bait presented on the drop is the ideal way of coming to grips with the rudd and roach inhabiting this huge, reed-lined, lily-covered lake.

work. Otherwise a 13 ft suffices. To facilitate a quick change, the swivel, push-in float attachment allows you to change from a tipped to a straight waggler (to improve visibility at distance). For rough conditions, select a bodied waggler for greater stability (fig. 16C).

When offering large baits like a bunch of maggots, sweetcorn, stewed wheat or bread flake, tie hooks direct to the reel line (see Hooks, p. 50). For a more delicate approach, especially in clear water, use a 1½ lb hook-length and hooks in sizes 16 and smaller for maggots and casters.

It is easy to overfeed roach and rudd, so unless shoals are truly enormous limit the loose feed to hook-bait fragments only, rather than heavy cereal feed, and introduce it regularly by catapult. A few small balls of cereal feed to get them interested is fine, but thereafter loose-fed casters or maggots fed little and often will suffice.

To reach distant, deep water the peacock loaded waggler, with its built-in weight at the base, will get your bait there. The equivalent of 2 to 4 swan shot wagglers are available according to distances you need to cover. And because so little shot is required down the line, it will allow the bait to be presented delicately.

As can be seen in fig. 17 A and B, it is shotted in exactly the same way as the tipped waggler to register bites both on the drop and on the bottom. In really deep swims

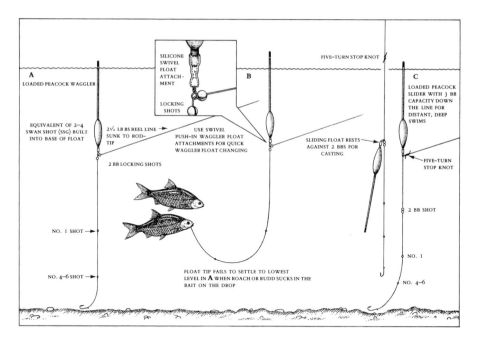

FIGURE 17 *Stillwater loaded peacock waggler/slider rigs*

during the summer months, when roach and rudd especially occupy the upper water layers, start with the float set to just 3 ft deep, and deepen off a foot or so every cast until bites come. The loaded waggler is a great float to use slider fashion where depths in excess of 10–12 ft present problems with the fixed float. For a loaded slider that accepts an additional shotting of 3BB down the line, for instance as in fig. 17C, split this up into three groups 18 in apart above the hook so the float rests against the 2BB for casting (fig. 17C).

Remember not to close the bale arm immediately after casting in order for line to peel off as the lower shots take the bait down through the bottom of the float. Remember also that once the slider knot hits against the bottom of the float, bites on the drop will be indicated if the tip fails to settle at its lowest position on time. It will in fact settle in three increments. When the 2BBs hang, when the No. 1 shot hangs, and finally when the No. 4 or 6 shots hang. Learn to count each down accordingly, striking instantly at anything out of the ordinary. If fish are layered in large shoals in that 3 or 4 ft band of water immediately above the bottom, you will experience a far greater proportion of bites on the drop than when fish are lying higher in the water.

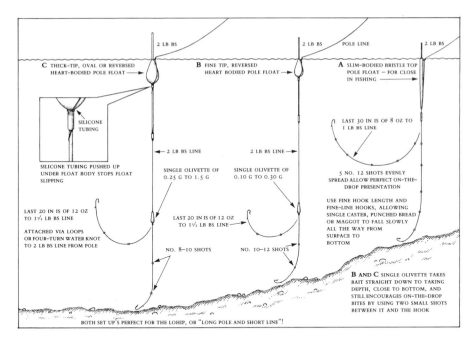

The following labels appear within the figure:

2 LB BS • 2 LB BS • POLE LINE • 2 LB BS

C THICK-TIP, OVAL OR REVERSED HEART-BODIED POLE FLOAT →

B FINE TIP, REVERSED HEART BODIED POLE FLOAT →

A SLIM-BODIED BRISTLE TOP POLE FLOAT – FOR CLOSE IN FISHING →

SILICONE TUBING

LAST 30 IN IS OF 8 OZ TO 1 LB BS LINE

SILICONE TUBING PUSHED UP UNDER FLOAT BODY STOPS FLOAT SLIPPING

← 2 LB BS LINE

2 LB BS LINE →

SINGLE OLIVETTE OF 0.25 G TO 1.5 G

SINGLE OLIVETTE OF 0.10 G TO 0.30 G

5 NO. 12 SHOTS EVENLY SPREAD ALLOW PERFECT ON-THE-DROP PRESENTATION

LAST 20 IN IS OF 12 OZ TO 1½ LB BS LINE

ATTACHED VIA LOOPS OR FOUR-TURN WATER KNOT TO 2 LB BS LINE FROM POLE

LAST 20 IN IS OF 12 OZ TO 1½ LB BS LINE

USE FINE HOOK LENGTH AND FINE-LINE HOOKS, ALLOWING SINGLE CASTER, PUNCHED BREAD OR MAGGOT TO FALL SLOWLY ALL THE WAY FROM SURFACE TO BOTTOM

NO. 8–10 SHOTS

NO. 10–12 SHOTS

B AND C SINGLE OLIVETTE TAKES BAIT STRAIGHT DOWN TO TAKING DEPTH, CLOSE TO BOTTOM, AND STILL ENCOURAGES ON-THE-DROP BITES BY USING TWO SMALL SHOTS BETWEEN IT AND THE HOOK

BOTH SET UP'S PERFECT FOR THE LOHIP, OR "LONG POLE AND SHORT LINE"!

FIGURE 18 *Stillwater pole float rigs*

Stillwater pole fishing

As I mentioned in the tackle chapter, presentation of the bait directly beneath the pole tip is second to none. Tackle rigs are not really so different from running-line set ups except that shots are not used close to the float.

To offer a small bait, caster or maggot, on the drop to summer rudd, which love the warmer upper water layers, or to super-wary roach or dace in a clear water canal, the set-up in fig. 18A is perfect. Using a slim-bodied bristle-top float, spread enough No. 12 shots evenly down the line (shirt-button style) so that only the merest tip of the bristle remains above the surface when the lowest shot hangs. If a bite does not happen on the drop or when the bait has been touching bottom for a while, it is easy with the pole to move the float (and thus the bait) several inches either to the right or left, or whisk it up off the bottom a couple of feet and let it fall again, or to lift the rig out completely, flipping it straight back in again to encourage bites on the drop. Plummeting of the swim is critical during the winter months when the fishes' metabolism has slowed down and bites are gentle dips of the fine tip. Most will come in that narrow band of water immediately above the bottom, and that is exactly where your bait needs to be all the time. The rig in fig. 18B is ideal because the single olivette takes the bait straight down, and the two tiny shots between it and the hook will still register on-the-drop bites. When fishing out a fair way into very deep water two things are needed – a float tip thick enough to be seen easily and a heavy enough olivette to take the bait straight down to the feeding zone (as in fig. 18C). Again, by using two tiny shots between the olivette and the hook, on-the-drop bites will register by the tip not settling properly, so watch it like a hawk. Whether summer or winter fishing, if the occasional specimen roach or rudd is on the cards among much smaller fish, and superlight tackle is imperative to initiate bites, use the elasticated tip set-up (see Pole tips, p. 59).

FLOAT FISHING IN RUNNING WATER

Pole fishing

To present the bait at reasonably close range or in gentle currents, the rig in fig. 19A, utilizing a heart-shaped or round-bodied wire stem float carrying somewhere between 0.030 and 1.50 g, will cover most situations. Presentation is far superior with the long pole/short line technique provided that roach or dace are situated no further out than, say, 11 yd.

There will be numerous occasions – when trotting the float way beyond the pole tip alongside trailing branches on the opposite bank of a small river, for instance, or fishing along the centre bowl of a canal into water 12–14 ft deep – that demand that you fish with a full pole-length of line out. Then, when you swing in a small fish, or the hook for re-baiting, they come directly 'to hand' – hence the terminology.

When fishing into really deep water, the 'to hand' method is extremely effective and much quicker than unshipping the pole after each cast to unhook or re-bait, although with an excess of line between float and pole tip, the sensitivity of the presentation can be impaired in strong

winds. When presentation to hand becomes totally impossible, think about swapping over to the waggler or a feeder outfit. Or try drawing the shoal closer in by feeding along a shorter line so the long pole/short line method can be employed.

The beauty of using the pole in running water is that you

Whenever the water is deep enough, 'fishing to hand' with a full pole-length of line out enables small fish to be swung in easily. Note how Terry Smith supports the butt of his II m pole in his groin.

Without question, the 'long pole – short line' technique, which utilizes a minimal length of line between pole-tip and float, permits the most accurate and sensitive bait presentation to dace, roach and to rudd, the species that Ian Heaps is seeking from this pretty Irish river.

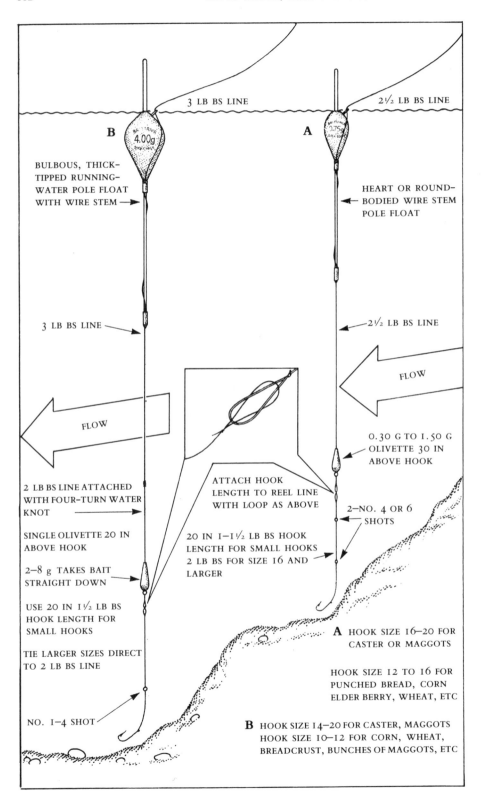

3 LB BS LINE

2½ LB BS LINE

B

A

BULBOUS, THICK-
TIPPED RUNNING-
WATER POLE FLOAT
WITH WIRE STEM →

← HEART OR ROUND-
BODIED WIRE STEM
POLE FLOAT

3 LB BS LINE →

← 2½ LB BS LINE

FLOW

FLOW

0.30 G TO 1.50 G
OLIVETTE 30 IN
ABOVE HOOK

ATTACH HOOK
LENGTH TO REEL LINE
WITH LOOP AS ABOVE

2 LB BS LINE ATTACHED
WITH FOUR-TURN WATER
KNOT →

2–NO. 4 OR 6
SHOTS

20 IN 1–1½ LB BS HOOK
LENGTH FOR SMALL HOOKS
2 LB BS FOR SIZE 16 AND
LARGER

SINGLE OLIVETTE 20 IN
ABOVE HOOK

2–8 g TAKES BAIT
STRAIGHT DOWN →

USE 20 IN 1½ LB BS
HOOK LENGTH FOR
SMALL HOOKS

A HOOK SIZE 16–20 FOR
CASTER OR MAGGOTS

TIE LARGER SIZES DIRECT
TO 2 LB BS LINE

HOOK SIZE 12 TO 16 FOR
PUNCHED BREAD, CORN
ELDER BERRY, WHEAT, ETC

NO. 1–4 SHOT

B HOOK SIZE 14–20 FOR CASTER, MAGGOTS
HOOK SIZE 10–12 FOR CORN, WHEAT,
BREADCRUST, BUNCHES OF MAGGOTS, ETC

can hold back gently on the bulbous-bodied float to slow the rig down and trundle the bait naturally through the swim really close to the bottom, like the loose-feed fragments.

FIGURE 19 *Running-water pole float rigs – long pole, short line or to hand*

Choose the size of float required to combat the current speed (always go heavier rather than lighter), and a simple bottom rig as shown in fig. 19 to deliver the bait straight down to the feeding zone – that first foot of water immediately above the bottom. Fix the single olivette around 20 in above the hook, with a No. 1 to No. 4 shot midway between. If the shot is moved closer to the hook, this will sometimes improve bite registration, so do not be afraid to move it around. In really cold water, hook sizes 14 to 20 go well with casters and maggots, while during the summer months especially, when you want to interest the larger fish (the main reason for offering the bait close to the bottom), hooks in sizes 10–12 will suit corn, wheat, bread or bunches of maggots.

If you find accurate groundbaiting rather difficult when fishing at 9–11 yd out, try touching the surface with the pole tip and use this as a marker when employing the 'long pole/short line' technique. Loose feed such as maggots, casters and hempseed are always best catapulted (leave the pole tip in the water, freeing both hands for catapulting). To ensure that it arrives around the hookbait when trotting in really deep water, either lock the casters or maggots up in a small ball of firmly-squeezed breadcrumb groundbait (see Groundbait, p. 84) that won't break up until it touches bottom, or use a small wire-mesh bait dropper. The latter are really effective for loose-feeding bait such as casters and maggots, except when you are using an elasticated tip (see Bait droppers, p. 64).

When easing the bait slowly through the water, concentrate on holding the pole really steady so that the float is not lifted or jerked. This is best achieved by holding it either across your knee or with the butt end lodged between crotch and seat, your strongest hand supporting it in front at arm's reach. This sounds more painful than it is, and it adds a couple of valuable feet to the pole's maximum distance with the fixed line. In fact, when fishing to hand, the butt of the pole remains lodged in the same position throughout and becomes the fulcrum for easy casting and playing.

Waggler fishing

During my early teens I used to buy bunches of peacock quills from the bird-house keeper at London Zoo or, when available, from the local tackle shop, and after carefully removing the herl I cut them down into 8 in lengths. I then gave them a ½ in band of fluorescent, matt red paint at one end, and kept them safe in a plastic tube in my tackle bag. At the water I simply slipped a ¼ in band of suitable-diameter silicone tubing on to the line, inserted a length of quill and pinched on the shotting capacity required to fish the current speed and depth of the intended swim. Then, using a pair of scissors, I trimmed the unpainted end of the quill (a little at a time) until the shots sunk the tip down to leave the desired amount showing above the surface.

I use this simple, quick and extremely effective procedure to this day when lift fishing with plain peacock quill. However, commercial wagglers, as they are now called, have neat bottom eyes, which permits a speedy change from one float to another with the help of a silicone float adapter (which is sleeved on to the line), making the plain old peacocks almost a thing of the past. In addition, because the bulk shot is grouped either side of the waggler, locking it in the desired position (remember to leave a ¾ in gap between these shots), not only does it cast accurately, like an arrow, but it 'folds' easily, flat to the line on the strike and so does not impair hook penetration.

A 2 or 2½ lb reel-line is perfect for all waggler fishing, used in conjunction with 13 ft waggler rod and a simple shotting pattern for slow currents (as shown in fig. 20A). The bulk shot for casting range in BBs (or AAs) is locked well over depth around the float with a succession of small shots, Nos. 4 or 6, dotted down the line every 18 in, shirt-button style, finishing with a tiny dust shot 18–20 in from the hook.

A single maggot or caster dragged slowly along the bottom (provided it is not littered with debris), just like all the loose feed, creates a wonderfully natural presentation to roach and dace, in both summer and winter. In deep, strongly pulling water use a waggler with a much heavier shotting capacity, most of which should be divided between the float and approximately mid depth, leaving a BB or No. 1 plus a 6 or 8 above the hook, as in fig. 20B.

When easing the waggler or stick float through freezing cold water to roach and dace, the bait needs to be presented well over depth so it trundles slowly along the bottom. Bites will consist of extremely gentle dips of the float, so ensure that the tip is shotted down to the merest 'dot' on the surface.

When long trotting in strong currents or in the deep, heavy water of big rivers after roach of this stamp, which prefer the bait to be eased through slowly, you need a float that carries plenty of shot down the line. John's brother, David Wilson, used a 6AA Avon float to combat the swirling waters of Trowse Mill Pool on Norfolk's tidal River Yare.

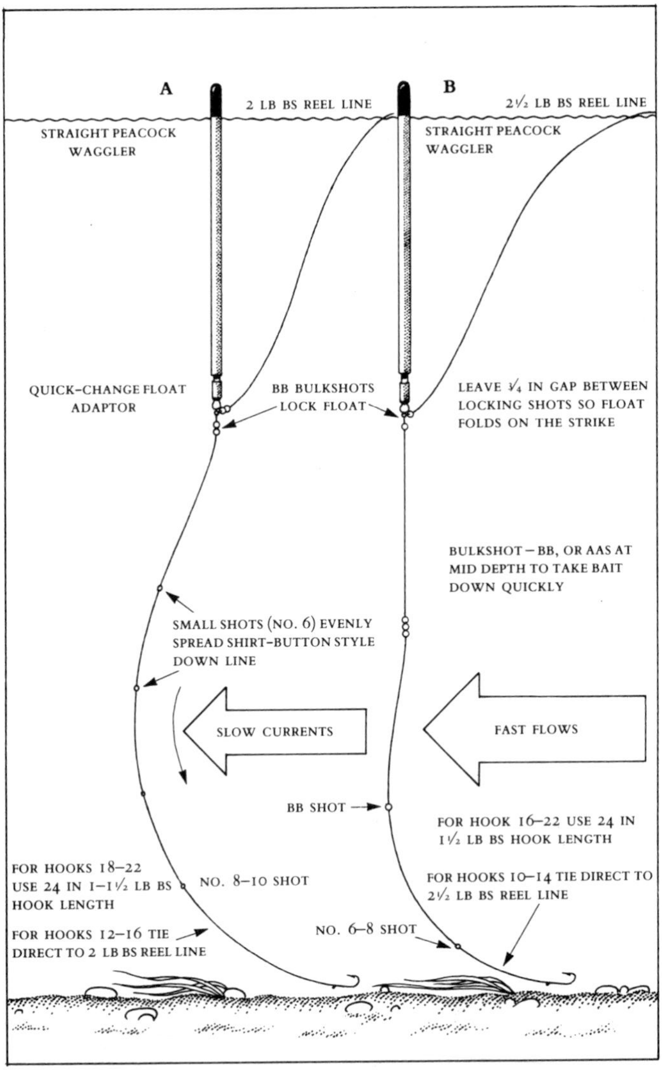

FIGURE 20 *The waggler in running water*

You will find that a single caster or maggot always fishes best. Larger offerings are naturally heavier and consequently catch repeatedly on the bottom when fished well over depth. To alleviate this problem, keep repositioning the float lower on each cast until the bait trots slowly through without fouling.

To ensure that the bait trundles smoothly through the swim, do not attempt to control the float as you might a stick float, for instance (see Stick-float fishing, p. 117). Simply allow line to peel freely from the reel unchecked and follow the float's passage downstream. For this to happen, the line must float and a rub with solid mucilin floatant for several yards immediately above the waggler helps enormously. Should the line start sinking, the float's progress can only be curtailed, the bait subsequently pulling away from the line you have been feeding.

When putting the waggler through really slow water in gale force winds, I will even contradict everything I have just written and deliberately sink the line in order to combat impossible conditions. But such times are rare. Ensure that the line floats well and the bait will behave naturally.

When trotting at long range, the bow of line on the surface created by the current could become so large that hook penetration might be impaired on even a hard, sweeping strike. Whenever this happens, hold the rod up high and flick the line back upstream again – an easy operation if the line is floating.

Stick-float fishing

Just as fishing the waggler fixed at its bottom end only requires a specialized technique, so does presentation of the bait beneath a stick float and all other floats of similar format that are fixed to the line both top and bottom with silicone tubing.

The reason for fixing a float top and bottom is one of control. As the line is not actually threaded through any part of the float, changing from one float to another is accomplished in a matter of seconds. However, over all it is the sensitivity in control of the stick float and the subsequent finesse in presentation of small baits like casters, maggots, hempseed, elderberries and tares, that sets the technique apart. Indeed, fishing the stick float should be considered a technique that only really works effectively at short range – certainly no further than an underarm flick of the tackle: for argument's sake, a distance of one and a half rod lengths or a distance beyond which loose feed cannot accurately be thrown by hand.

As soon as you try to control a float cast any further, it will be pulled away from the line being fed and at which the shoal is lying, as it is taken downstream by the current. So first and foremost, think of presenting the stick to roach

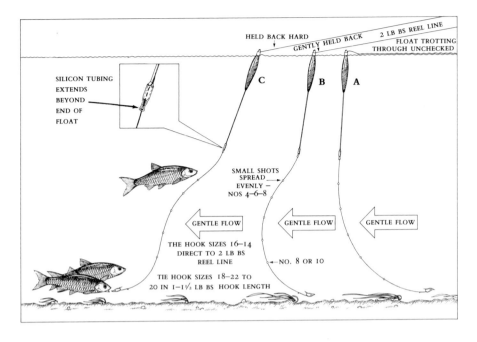

FIGURE 21 *Fishing the stick float*

and dace occupying marginal and close-range swims only. Beyond this, use the waggler.

Consider the basic shotting pattern of the wire-stemmed stick float, for instance, in fig. 21. The reel-line is 2 lb, and hooks in sizes 18–22 are tied to a finer, 20 in length of 1–1½ lb test. Small shots, Nos. 4, 6 or 8 (depending on the capacity of the particular float) are spread evenly shirt-button style down the line, with a single dust shot around 20 in above the hook.

Sometimes bites happen when the float is trotted along, as usual set well over depth and completely unchecked, as in fig. 21. More bites, however, are usually instigated by constant light-fingered control of the stick float. This is why I prefer to use the centre-pin reel, because line is taken from the drum directly, without any jerks – impossible with open-faced and fixed-spool reels. Bites also happen when you gently hold back, as in fig. 21B, which momentarily speeds up the bait's forward movement. And by holding back hard for several seconds, as in fig. 21C, the bait is whisked off the bottom to flutter enticingly ahead of the float. Dace, especially, are really attracted to this action, and your reflexes need to be sharp.

For a really slow search of the swim, particularly effective in cold water conditions when roach are loathe to give chase, slightly overshot the float so that if left to trot through unchecked, the tip would actually disappear. Of course, by gently controlling and holding back on the tip, it keeps just above the surface to indicate the very slightest and most hesitant of bites instantly. A single, buoyant caster presented slowly just above bottom in conjunction with hempseed fed very sparingly is a wonderful winter combination for both roach and dace. An elderberry or tare on the hook plus loose-fed hemp is also a winner (see Baits, p. 76).

The stick float, or spliced tip, rod was in fact created to permit such sensitive and delicate control of light float tackle. Persevere with the technique and you will obtain enormous pleasure from catching roach and dace of all sizes.

Fishing big sticks, balsa trotters and Avons

Presentation of the bait beneath these three floats, which have a much larger shotting capacity than the stick float (up to 6AA in the case of Avons), is almost an extension of stick-float fishing. When trotting big floats a long way downstream, the waggler rod is the tool to use.

Each float is fixed securely at the top and bottom with silicone tubing, and controlled in exactly the same way. Reel line may be increased to 2½ lb for the heavier balsa trotters and Avons. And when offering big baits such as a lump of bread flake, a cube of crust or a bunch of maggots or casters, with specimen roach in mind, hooks are best tied direct.

Otherwise, it is all about choosing the right float for the current speed and the depth of the swim being fished. For instance, if currents are swirling with the surface patterns deviating every so often, even a big stick, which slips under all too easily, is not going to present the bait steadily enough. So the obvious set up is shown in fig. 22C, incorporating an oval-bodied Avon, which is used with most of the bulk shot set around mid depth. This ensures that the bait gets down quickly and stays there throughout the trot, close to the bottom where the roach are holding.

In currents of less force, the balsa trotter rig shown in fig. 22B works well in both shallow and deep runs, and its

FIGURE 22 *Fishing
big sticks – balsa
trotters – Avons*

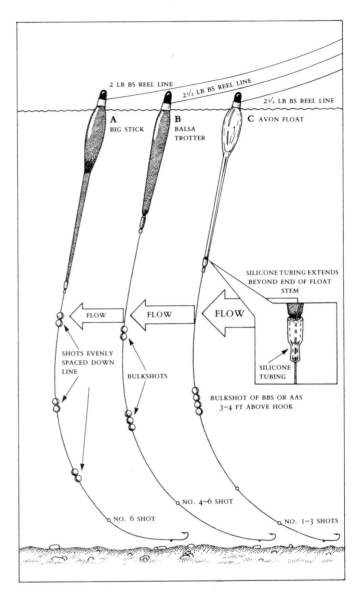

wide tip is easy to see, even at distances of up to 25 yd. This is a good, all-round, heavy-water float choice.

In strong, steady water, the big stick rig shown in fig. 22A, with the shotting load evenly distributed, will present the bait both slowly and sensitively. It can be overshotted and gently eased along just like smaller, lighter sticks but, and this applies to all three floats, control is still only really effective at distances up to one and a half rod lengths out. The distance downstream is not important because the further the float travels, the more in line it will be with the rod tip. But when cast straight out from the angler, any kind of control will only pull the bait off the feed line. I cannot stress this heavily enough.

Stret pegging

Last and by no means least among running-water float-fishing techniques, we come to the art of stret pegging. This, being a mixture of float ledgering and laying on, is a technique for ensuring the bait is placed accurately at close range and lies perfectly static on the bottom.

FIGURE 23 *Stret pegging*

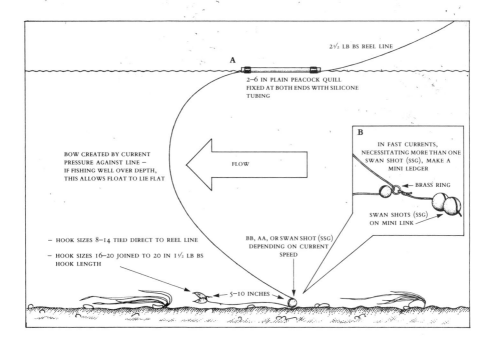

2½ LB BS REEL LINE

A

2–6 IN PLAIN PEACOCK QUILL FIXED AT BOTH ENDS WITH SILICONE TUBING

B

IN FAST CURRENTS, NECESSITATING MORE THAN ONE SWAN SHOT (SSG), MAKE A MINI LEDGER

BOW CREATED BY CURRENT PRESSURE AGAINST LINE – IF FISHING WELL OVER DEPTH, THIS ALLOWS FLOAT TO LIE FLAT

FLOW

BRASS RING

SWAN SHOTS (SSG) ON MINI LINK

– HOOK SIZES 8–14 TIED DIRECT TO REEL LINE

– HOOK SIZES 16–20 JOINED TO 20 IN 1½ LB BS HOOK LENGTH

BB, AA, OR SWAN SHOT (SSG) DEPENDING ON CURRENT SPEED

5–10 INCHES

As long as roach or dace are occupying a deepish run close in to the bank beside man-made pilings, alongside marginal sedges or reeds, natural lay-bys and so on, then almost regardless of the flow, stret pegging is the only way of watching a float with the bait laid hard on. It is a superb method in both summer and winter, especially during exceptionally cold conditions when roach and dace are loathe to chase a moving bait. As can be seen from fig. 23A, the float (a short length of unpainted peacock quill)

For presenting the bait completely static on the bottom in strong currents with a float on the surface to watch, there is no more effective and delightful way than stret pegging. Andy Davison puts the method to good use for the dace inhabiting this shallow pool on Norfolk's River Tud, where continual trotting of the bait only spooks the shoal.

needs to be fixed top and bottom and set considerably more than swim depth so the current forms a bow in the line between the float and the bottom shots. This to some extent relieves pressure on the float, enabling it to lie flat, and the bait to remain static with just a single BB, AA or swan shot (depending on current force) pinched on the line 5–10 in from the hook.

The reel line should be 2½ lb test (in conjunction with a 13 ft waggler rod), and as I generally use this technique for catching specimen roach, hooks in sizes 8–14 are tied direct for baits like bread flake and crust or stewed wheat. When after modest-sized fish, and there is a need to step down much lighter, such as in clear, cold water conditions, add a 20 in length of 1½ lb test, permitting hooks in sizes 16–20 to be used with smaller baits like maggots and casters.

When the flow is exceptionally strong, too fast for a

single shot to hold bottom, construct a mini ledger using a small ring plus 1 in or so of thick line, to which two or three swan shots are added, as in fig. 23B.

Always sit looking down river and make the cast directly downstream and across so the rig swings inwards. Put the rod on two rests with the tip angled upwards so no line actually lies on the surface, or the float may be swept under. Most bites are positive, with the float simply gliding under, sometimes preceeded by a gentle twitching or shaking. When presenting bread flake, introduce a few balls of mashed bread well upstream, allowing for current speed, so it comes to rest close to the hookbait. With maggots and casters, use a bait dropper to deposit them with accuracy in strong currents or deep water.

Stret pegging is a great flood-water technique, when rivers run tea-coloured and lap the banks, and the shoals of roach and dace fill the choice slacks or move into the mouths of sidestreams where they join the main river. Put down a couple of bait droppers full of maggots or casters and follow in with your stret-pegging rig. In mild weather, you will not wait long for a bite. In cold weather, if the maggots come back sucked to skins without any noticeable registration on the float, reduce the hook length to just 3 or 4 in – it makes all the difference when fish are not moving off with the bait but lying there chewing it on the spot.

FLY FISHING

Dace

Dace are forever willing to suck in artificials, and because they rise to the dry fly so quickly, they are actually more difficult to catch than trout. This provides a wonderful challenge on a lightweight dry-fly outfit (see Tackle, p. 46), requiring a leader point of no more than 2 lb. In fact, when presenting tiny size 18 dry flies, I taper the leader down to a 1½ lb point.

The splashy surface movements of dace are easily seen at the tail end of shallow runs and pools, where several fish might all hit the surface together during a prolific hatch.

You can match the hatch of natural insects or present any small patterns and expect to see some action, so long as the fly is gently put down just upstream of the shoal on a snaky line so it does not drag. Remember to grease the cast well, and make use of any available bankside cover to creep into a casting position a little downstream of the rising shoal. You cannot wait a second or two, as you must with trout, for the fish to get its head well down. Dace rise to and eject that fly like greased lightning. So you must strike and pull into them with equal speed.

Presentation of the dry fly is a super way of tempting really big dace inhabiting clear, shallow streamy runs where they repeatedly refuse baits on float tackle because presentation is difficult due to the extreme shallowness of the water. And this is the real beauty of using the fly rod to catch roach, rudd and dace, because they can be extracted from spots where no other method will work.

Wherever dace are not interested in accepting the dry fly on the surface, try them on a slowly sinking nymph. Grease all but the last 2 or 3 ft of the cast and offer a size 16 leaded shrimp or pheasant tail. Cast it upstream to the head of the run, watching the ungreased line sink as the flow brings the nymph downstream towards you. Any sudden twitch, jerk or obvious slow pull should be instantly met with a firm pull on the line with your left hand (assuming you hold the rod in your right) and a lift of the rod. Dace also take the wet fly when it is presented in the traditional manner downstream and across on a wet line, but are far more sporting on a dry-line outfit.

Roach

Roach lack the agility of the dace but are wily. They are also most partial to a slowly sinking nymph. Grease the cast to within 2 or 3 ft of a slightly weighted nymph if fishing a shallow river (4 to 6 ft for stillwaters), and watch like a hawk as the tip of the cast descends, striking at any unnatural movement.

Where possible, try to identify what is actually being taken and match it with something from your box. Alternatively, where roach are known to inhabit a certain spot but are not rising regularly, offer a size 14 or 16 leaded shrimp, a sedge pupa or a pheasant tail nymph.

In deep, steady pools a much larger artificial, such as a heavily leaded mayfly nymph, will attract roach. Size 12 and 10 are not too large, and remember to use a leader point of no less than 2½ lb.

Rudd

During those really warm, sultry days of summer, rudd are readily fooled at the surface with small dry flies. And as the artificial could be floating for some time in stillwaters, I prefer the extra buoyancy of winged patterns like the coachman, alder and small red sedge, on size 14 and 16 hooks tied to a 2 lb point, well rubbed in mucilin.

Where rudd exist in numbers, the disturbance they cause at the surface, swirling after hatching aquatic flies, can be relied upon as the sun starts to set. And this, incidentally, is when specimen rudd move close in to the margins in large lakes and pits, putting the chances of a whopper on the dry fly quite within your grasp.

Rudd might also rise at any time of the day, even in bright sunshine, whenever there is a hatch, but they are more likely to be located basking around the trailing branches of overhanging willows and beneath large lily patches. A dry fly delicately presented close by is rarely refused, but even more deadly is a slowly sinking nymph. As rudd obtain most of their natural food during the summer months from the upper water layers, a pheasant tail, shrimp, sedge pupa or corixa plopped deliberately beside a lily-pad or overhanging branches, and allowed to sink slowly, promotes really positive takes. The cast shoots dramatically across the surface as a rudd inhales the artificial and darts immediately away lest other shoal members attempt to get in on the act.

A favourite oddball method that I favour and practise regularly in the summer, when rudd and roach are visible through the clear water of estate lakes, pits and weedy, slow-moving rivers, but are not rising, is to put the shoal into a feeding mood by creating my own hatch and regularly catapulting out maggots. Once fish are freely accepting each maggot as it descends (you can, with practice, even work the shoal into a feeding frenzy on the

Above: *Fly-fishing for roach, rudd and dace not only opens up a whole new world of enjoyment, it also allows you to approach and attract fish inhabiting difficult spots that cannot be taken by any other technique, like the roach inhabiting the far run on this weedy river. The water is no more than 1 ft deep.*

Right: *The dry fly is effective for rudd and dace, which rise freely if approached with caution. Dace are more difficult to hook consistently than the brown trout, and provide a wonderful challenge.*

surface), I tie a size 16 or 14 hook to the end of the cast and nick on firmly a couple of maggots. Provided that the casting is not fierce, only occasionally does one come off (hence the reason for putting two on) and you have the option of watching the maggot slowly sink or the cast for indications of a take – or both. Give it a try; it is a fun technique for roach, rudd and dace.

Good fishing

INDEX